NOSH

FOR BUSY MUMS & DADS

by Joy May AND the family team

NEW

NOSH FOR STUDENTS
5TH EDITION
PHOTO WITH EVERY RECIPE
A FUN STUDENT COOKBOOK
OVER 100,000 STUDENT NOSH BOOKS SOLD
JOY MAY

ISBN: 9780993260933

NOSH FOR STUDENTS
VOL.2
THE SEQUEL TO 'NOSH FOR STUDENTS'...GET THE OTHER ONE FIRST!
OVER 300,000 STUDENT NOSH BOOKS SOLD
JOY MAY

ISBN: 9780956746467

NEW

VEGETARIAN NOSH FOR STUDENTS
3RD EDITION
PHOTO WITH EVERY RECIPE
A FUN STUDENT COOKBOOK
OVER 300,000 STUDENT NOSH BOOKS SOLD
JOY MAY

ISBN: 9780993260940

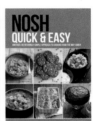

NOSH QUICK & EASY
ANOTHER...VERY FAMILIALLY SIMPLE, APPROACH TO COOKING FROM THE MAY FAMILY
JOY MAY

ISBN: 9780956746481

NOSH FOR BUSY MUMS & DADS
A FAMILY COOKBOOK WITH EVERYDAY FOOD FOR REAL FAMILIES.
AUTHOR OF BEST SELLING COOKBOOK 'NOSH FOR STUDENTS'
JOY MAY

ISBN: 9780956746443

NOSH GLUTEN-FREE
A NO-FUSS, EVERYDAY GLUTEN-FREE COOKBOOK FROM THE MAY FAMILY
JOY MAY

ISBN: 9780956746450

NOSH GLUTEN-FREE BAKING
ANOTHER NO-FUSS, GLUTEN-FREE COOKBOOK FROM THE MAY FAMILY
JOY MAY

ISBN: 9780956746498

NOSH SUGAR-FREE GLUTEN-FREE
SAYING 'NO' TO PROCESSED SUGAR AND GLUTEN IN OUR TESTED GF DISHES
JOY MAY

ISBN: 9780993260919

@NOSHBOOKS

WE WOULD LOVE TO HEAR FROM YOU. USE

#NOSHBOOKS

contents

introduction 3

basics 16

weekly menus 34

quick bites 39

everyday fast food 55

something for the weekend 89

old classics 119

special days 145

kids' parties 159

getting kids involved 165

budget days 183

cakes & cookies 207

yummy desserts 233

index 248

introduction

My sons have left home now, but visit frequently, with their children, so I am now a busy Gran. I remember well the pressures of juggling work with bringing up children, looking after the home, cooking, etc. Add this to a tight budget and busy husband, who was often not seen between 7.30 in the morning and 7.00 at night, cooking was a challenge. I always aimed to cook a meal for everyone, but it wasn't easy. I would have loved to have had a book like this one, to inspire me and help me through those times.

My aim in this book is to help those of you who are in the same place, to enjoy cooking, to minimize the stress, to see how simple meals are possible and to inspire you to cook from fresh ingredients. Sometimes we can get into the rut of cooking the same things over and over, or reaching for the ready-made meals. I have included recipes that should take under 30 minutes to produce and some that may take 10 minutes to prepare and then to sit in the oven for an hour or so. There are recipes that your kids can join in with and some especially designed for when the funds are low. All of these recipes should satisfy hungry tums.

For those of you with younger children, there are some tips on getting them to eat, not getting stressed when they don't, and some simple snacks for kids.

Fridge

butter

spreads

milk

eggs

cheese, good, strong and tasty

mayo

stock, concentrated or cubes

Freezer

spare loaf

packet of puff pastry

mince

chicken breast

peas

Cupboards

olive oil

sunflower oil

potatoes (in a bag)

onions (in a bag)

garlic (in a pot)

lemons

tinned tomatoes

tinned tuna

baked beans

cannellini beans

sweetcorn

tomato purée

sun-dried tomatoes

couscous

spaghetti

pasta

rice, basmati

lentils

tomato sauce

flour, self-raising and plain

Worcestershire sauce

balsamic vinegar

white wine vinegar

soy sauce

assorted curry pastes

salt and pepper

pilau rice seasoning

mixed dried herbs

cinnamon

cumin

ground coriander

ground ginger

turmeric

paprika

chilli powder

honey

raisins

vanilla extract

sugar, white brown and caster

fresh herbs, if you have a window sill!

Gluten-free

We recognise that there are more and more families dealing with allergies, such as gluten and wheat intolerances. For this reason, and the fact that we are fairly passionate about the whole subject of gluten, we have given some tips on how to adapt some of the recipes to avoid gluten and wheat products. In each recipe where you see the 'gluten-free option' icon, you will also see notes next to each ingredient which you need to make sure is gluten-free.

labour saving equipment

Food processor

I would highly recommend getting a large, good quality processor. It will mix, slice, grate, liquidise, whip, not quite 'sing and dance', but will save a lot of time and energy.

Hand-held blender

Great to get out quickly to liquidise soups, etc.

Food mixer

Handy for egg whites, pancakes, small cakes, etc. Saves aching arms.

Hob-to-oven casserole

Useful if you are cooking on the hob and later it goes in the oven. Saves washing-up a saucepan.

Good, thick bottomed saucepans

They are expensive, but will last for years and years. I have some and they are about 20 years old. They go in the dishwasher and come out as good as new.

2 non-stick frying pans

If you are making cooked breakfast or pancakes, having two frying pans makes life so much easier.

Long-handled plastic tongs

Get the ones with the silicon ends and they will save scraping the non-stick off the pans. They are so easy to turn over things with.

Non-stick wok

The food cooks quicker than in a large saucepan, as there is more surface heat.

Good silicon spatulas and cooking spoons

Much more hygienic than wooden spoons and easy to clean.

Good sharp knives.

Having a good sharp knife and a sharpener takes the labour out of chopping. Collect them gradually, as they can be expensive. A chopping, paring knife and carving knife are all you really need.

An easy-peeler

Don't keep using the one you have had for years. Buy a new, sharp one and take the toil out of any peeling you may feel necessary.

Good, sturdy, sharp grater

If yours is dull and floppy, it will take forever to grate cheese and your arm is left aching and tired.

A wooden and a plastic chopping board

Wood for normal stuff, plastic for fish or anything really smelly.

Teflon sheets

Cost around £3 and last for ages. Really sticky stuff comes off in seconds and you are not left soaking and scrubbing baking or roasting trays.

saving time

Easy measuring

Learn how to measure using spoons and mugs, or your hand! The recipes in the book give tablespoon, dessertspoon, teaspoon and mug measures. The mug is ½ pint. I keep a mug handy all the time I cook, much easier and quicker than using scales. The illustration on the next page shows the size of the mug.

Prepare well before you start

Gather together all your ingredients before you start cooking. This way, you won't be running around looking for things as you cook. Clear your working surfaces of as much 'stuff' as possible and just have the really important things out.

Half your time and effort

Cook double and freeze. If you know you want to use a meal from the freezer in the evening, get it out in the morning and leave in the fridge throughout the day. This way, it should be almost defrosted by the time you come to use it. Throughout the book I have noted the recipes which are good for freezing. Tips on freezing can be found on our website: noshbooks.com/freezing

Let the supermarket do the work

Buy groceries online. If I have a list, I can shop online in 10 minutes, whilst it takes an hour to go to the supermarket. You may want to go to the shops for an outing, but it takes time and energy. Delivery can be as little as £3.50 and it may cost you nearly that in petrol to get to the supermarket.

Don't waste time waiting for water to boil

Boil water for veggies, pasta or rice in the kettle, not the pan. Put the kettle on before you start cooking.

Short prep, long cook

Slow-cook recipes often require little preparation, just a long time in the oven, e.g. "Sweet Pork & Apple Stew" (page 102) and "Beef & Mushroom Casserole" (page 124).

Enlist help

Use spouses, friends or kids, if they can help. Be specific about what they can do, e.g. chop things, wash things up, set the table, etc. Get a step-up, or stool, so younger kids can be involved. Short term, kids may seem to get in the way, but, long term, they need to be able to cook and will be a help.

In the peace and quiet

If you have a small baby, cook when they are 'napping'. Much less frustrating than when they are awake and require your attention.

Buy things like pastry. When the children are older you will have a lifetime to make pastry, bread and all those 'homey' things.

What is quicker than just grabbing a mug and filling it? What is easier to remember as a unit of measure than a mug of this, or 2 mugs of that?

This book is designed so that you don't need to use weighing scales, but we have included the gram/millilitre measures for those of you who prefer a bit more precision.

Throughout the book I have used a mug to measure ingredients. This mug holds $1/2$ pint or 300ml of liquid and is the exact size of the mug pictured opposite. So find a mug that measures up to this one and you won't go far wrong.

This actual mug is the same one I used when writing my first book back in 2000. It has a place in my heart. Although it is now cracked, it still has a special spot in our mug cupboard!

a mug =

ACTUAL SIZE

saving money

Shop at Costco/Makro

These are big, wholesale supermarkets. If you don't qualify, you can get a card on a friend's account. You need to buy in bulk, but many things are significantly cheaper. Buy in bulk when things are on offer in the supermarket.

Make soups

This is inexpensive and and provides a substantial, tasty meal.

Buy spices in bulk

Buy the refill bags and store in airtight jars. They will keep for ages. The Natco brand is available at Sainsbury's, most Asian supermarkets and online at www. natco-online.com

Make your own packed lunches

Make for yourselves and for the children. To make a wholemeal bread, ham, lettuce and mayo sandwich costs approximately 88p in total. To buy a ready-made ham salad sandwich is around £2. This is a saving of £5.60 per week per person. See 'packed lunches' section on page 30.

Use things up at the end of the week

At the end of the week, use the veg that's coming towards the end of its life in dishes like "Roasted Sweet Potato Soup" (see page 44), or "Chicken and Roast Vegetable Couscous" (see page 66).

Freeze leftovers

If you just have enough left for one portion, freeze it. Save up the single portions till you have enough for everyone to have their choice and you have a 'no cook' night.

Bread

Put whole, sliced loaves in the freezer and only get bread out when you need it, as it is so quick to defrost. This way you don't waste the dried-up slices and you always use fresh bread.

'Cost up' your weekly shop

If you have a tight budget each week, it might be helpful to plan your menu. To help you do that, we price up every meal in our books, so hopefully you won't have any surprises when you get to the till. The prices in this book are correct as of **February 2017** (ave. of Tesco and Sainsbury's). Every time we reprint any of our books, we aim to update the pricing.

How much should my child be eating?

Don't worry too much about how much they are eating; their appetite will vary. If they have a growth spurt, they may be more hungry. There is no definitive portion size. It is more important that they do not eat too much, or too much of the wrong kinds of food. Compare the size of your own fist and the child's; this gives an idea of the comparative proportion of your food and theirs. Give them food on a child's plate and this also will give an indication of the amount they need.

What if they won't eat?

Don't worry or think you are the only person whose child is fussy. Most under-fives tend to be picky at times with no reason.

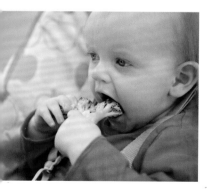

One of the best ways to get children to eat is for them to come to the table hungry. If they have eaten crisps, ice creams, chocolate and sweets, or had sweet drinks between meals, the 'food battle' will commence. Try to give these things as a treat, or reward for eating healthy food. Don't keep lots of sweets and crisps in the house, as this will reduce their availability.

Start young. You can give them blitzed-up portions of your meals if they are suitable. This way, they will get used to lots of different tastes. As young children should not be eating salt, etc., make sure that you add the seasoning after you have taken out their portion. This is also much less expensive than buying ready-prepared foods. As they begin to eat 'finger food', introduce as many new foods as possible.

Make food attractive

If everything is 'brown' or mushy, it's not too attractive. Broccoli, tomatoes, sweetcorn, etc. help to brighten up plates of food. Avoid large chunks of cooked mushroom and onion, as the texture can be off-putting. Chop these kinds of food up small, so they are disguised.

Make food tasty

This may seem obvious. One way to make veggies tasty is to roast them (see page 44). Soup that has been blitzed-up in a food processor (make sure it's a good colour) is a great way to get vegetables into children. Serve with some good crusty bread they can dip in the soup.

Don't overwhelm them with a large plate of food

Give them special children's plates. It is amazing what a fairy or car on a plate will do. Keep trying to introduce different foods and don't give up the first time they refuse. Get them to try at least one mouthful of something they have not already tried. Don't let them just say 'don't like it' without tasting it.

Reward them with praise and approval

when they eat all their food or try something new. Sticker charts work well. Find something that they really want, a DVD, new toy, etc. and set up a chart for one month. If they get five stickers on

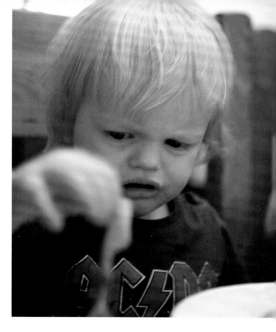

the chart every week, then they get the reward. You do not necessarily need to get them to eat everything on a plate, just a few mouthfuls of each type of food given.

Getting them involved in the cooking process

can also help. There are a few recipes in the book where I suggest that children can help, even from the toddler age. Pizzas are great, as they can make their own small one. It may seem time-consuming in the food prep stage, but, if it saves half an hour of frustration and tension at the meal table, it is worth it.

Make meal-times special

If possible eat together, as this way the children see their parents eating normally. This means that the Dads who still think broccoli are really small trees and should not be eaten will have to behave themselves!

Don't make food a battleground

if you have a strong-willed child they will just dig in their heels. Don't pressure, simply say things like "this is what we are eating. It is ok if you don't want it, but there will be nothing else until the next meal". Let them leave the table, BUT don't give them anything else, however much they plead. They will soon learn to eat what is there.

perfect rice *every* time

I would recommend that you use basmati rice, as it consistently cooks well.

Rice for 1 adult = $\frac{1}{2}$ mug rice + 1 mug water

(+ 1 teaspoon of pilau rice seasoning. Optional, but gives a yummy flavour)

1 Using a pan with a lid, bring the water to the boil, add the seasoning and stir.

2 Add the rice and stir once. Bring back to the boil. Once boiling, turn down to simmer gently. Put the lid on the pan and cook for approximately 15 minutes. Do not stir while the rice is cooking, or you will make it sticky.

3 Test the rice once the water has boiled away. If the rice is still too crunchy, and the water has all gone, then you have boiled it too quickly. Add a little more water, replace the lid and cook for another 5 minutes.

how to cook pasta

There are innumerable kinds of pasta to choose from in the shops, made from different ingredients. Most will have instructions on the packets as to how to cook them. Just in case you have lost the packet, here are some general guidelines:

spaghetti

1 Boil sufficient water in a pan to cover the spaghetti whilst cooking.

2 Once the water is boiling, lower the spaghetti sticks into the water. Once the half that is in the water has softened slightly, push the other half in. Simmer for 6–8 minutes.

3 Drain the water off and add one teaspoon of butter, or olive oil, to stop the spaghetti sticking together.

spaghetti measure

most other pastas

Again, boil enough water to cover the pasta. Once the water is boiling, add the pasta. One mug of dried pasta is plenty for one person with a very healthy appetite. Simmer for the appropriate time, drain and add butter, or olive oil, to prevent the pasta sticking together.

As a rough guide, here are some timings for various pastas:

Tagliatelle (4–5 mins)   **Conchiglie** (7–8 mins)

Radiatore (10 mins)   **Macaroni** (12–15 mins)

Fusilli (6–8 mins)   **Farfalle** (6–8 mins)

Penne (10–12 mins)

all things potatoes

Roast Potatoes

serves 4 if you use 6 medium potatoes

1 Preheat the oven to 180ºC fan oven/200ºC/Gas 6. Cut the potatoes into 2–3" chunks. You do not need to peel the potatoes.

2 Place them on a baking tray. Sprinkle with salt and oil. If you have some fresh rosemary, pull off the leaves and sprinkle over the potatoes (dried rosemary will also work fine).

3 Using your hands, make sure the oil is evenly distributed around the potatoes. Make sure that the potatoes are not flat side down, as this will mean more of the potatoes will brown.

4 Cook in the oven for 45–50 minutes until they are brown.

Mini Roast Potatoes

This a great way to make roast potatoes in a short time. They will cook in the time it takes to make the rest of a meal. Serves 4 if you use 6 medium potatoes.

1 Preheat the oven to 180ºC fan oven/200ºC/Gas 6.

2 Cut the potatoes into 1" cubes. You don't need to peel them.

3 Place them on a baking tray, drizzle oil over them and season with salt and pepper. Mix the oil and seasoning into the potatoes with your hands.

4 Place in the oven, for 25–30 minutes, until browned.

5 You can sprinkle some dried rosemary over the potatoes if you wish.

Amazing Wedges

1 Preheat the oven to 180ºC fan oven/200ºC/Gas 6 . Cut the potatoes into wedges.

2 Place on baking trays and sprinkle with oil and salt. Distribute the oil well with your hands.

3 Make sure that each wedge is 'standing up', not sitting on a flat side. You will get nice brown wedges this way and they won't stick to the tray as much.

4 Place in the oven for 25-30 minutes, or until browned.

Posh Roast Potatoes

serves 4 if you use 6 medium potatoes

1 Preheat the oven to 180ºC fan oven/200ºC/ Gas 6. Peel the potatoes and cut into 2-3" chunks.

2 Place in a pan of boiling water and cook for 10 minutes.

3 Place a baking tray in the oven with 2 tablespoons of vegetable oil on it.

4 Drain the potatoes and return to the pan. Put the lid on the pan and shake it quite vigorously. This will cause the outsides of the potatoes to become a little furry.

5 Place the potatoes on the heated baking tray and turn them to distribute the oil.

6 Put in the oven for 45-50 minutes, until browned.

Basic Mash

6 **medium potatoes**, peeled

25g cube **butter** (measure using packet)

salt and **pepper**

1   Cut the potatoes into 2" chunks.

2   Put the potatoes into boiling, salted water. Once the water has come back to the boil, turn down the heat, put a lid on the pan and cook for approximately 10 minutes.

3   Test after 10 minutes. If cooked, drain the water off. If not cooked, boil for a little longer, taking care not to overcook, or the potatoes will disintegrate in the water.

4   Add the butter and mash with a potato masher.

5   Mash until all the lumps have gone, but don't work the mash too much as it will become glutinous. Add salt and freshly ground pepper.

Potato Crush

6-8 **medium potatoes**

1   Put boiled water in a large saucepan. Bring back to the boil.

2   Cut unpeeled, washed potatoes into 2cm chunks. Add to the boiling water, season with salt and bring back to the boil. Cover with a lid and simmer for 10 minutes.

More Than Mash

'Mash' has had old-fashioned connotations for many years, but is making a definite comeback in modern cooking, rarely as 'simple mash'. Here are some ways to spice it up:

Cheddar and Mustard Mash

At the 'mashing stage', add $1/2$ mug grated, mature cheddar cheese, together with 1 good teaspoon of wholegrain mustard, salt and freshly ground black pepper. The wholegrain mustard also gives an attractive look to the mash.

Sweet Potato Mash

Just use half normal potatoes and half sweet potatoes.

3   Drain and return the potatoes to the pan.

4   Add a good chunk of butter. You can add a mug of grated cheese at this point. Use a potato masher and just squash the potatoes. Don't completely mash them, keep them 'rustic'. Stir with a spoon to distribute the butter and the cheese if you have used it. Put the lid back on the pan to keep warm until needed.

jacket potatoes

Jacket potatoes make a very easy meal. You can make them much more interesting than by just adding beans or cheese. Use medium or large potatoes. Always make a cut in the skin with a knife before baking, or it may explode in the oven or the microwave. You will only get the crisp jackets, if you cook the potato in the oven. Timing depends on the size of the potato.

Oven baked – Preheat the oven to 200ºC fan/220ºC/gas 7 and bake for 50 minutes to 1 hour.

Microwave and oven – Preheat the oven to 200ºC fan/220ºC/gas 7. Cook in the microwave on full power for 5 minutes and then in the oven for 30 minutes.

Microwave – 7-10 minutes on full power.

the fillings

Bacon and Beans

Fry 6 **smoked bacon rashers** until they are crisp. Remove from the pan and chop into small strips (scissors work well for this). Chop an **onion** and fry until it begins to brown. Add to one **tin of beans**, together with 1 teaspoon **brown sugar** and 1 tablespoon **Worcestershire sauce**. Serves 4.

Sweet Potato Bakes

Bake in the same way as normal potatoes. Mix together ½ x 200g pack of **feta cheese** with 3 chopped **spring onions**, ½ a **fat red chilli**, deseeded and chopped, zest of a **lemon** and 2 chopped **tomatoes**. Season well and share amongst the potatoes. Serves 2-3.

Tuna, Sweetcorn and Mayo

Mix together a **tin of tuna** with 1 tablespoon of **mayo** and a 340g tin of **sweetcorn**. Season well. Serves 4. Any leftovers can be used in sandwiches.

Cooked Chicken and Mayonnaise

Pan roast a couple of **chicken breasts** (see page 66). One minute before the end of the cooking time, spread a dessertspoon of **curry paste** over the chicken. Slice the chicken and mix with 1 tablespoon of **mayo** and 2 chopped **spring onions**. Serves 4.

Salami and Red Pepper

Chop 3 slices of not-too-spicy **salami** plus 1 **ready-roasted, red pepper** (from a jar) and 2 tablespoons **crème fraîche**. Serves 2-3.

Salmon and Soured Cream

Mix a 120g packet of **smoked salmon trimmings** with a 300g pot of **soured cream** and 1 tablespoon of **freshly chopped mixed herbs** (basil works fine on its own). Season with **salt** and **pepper** and share between the potatoes. Serves 4.

stuff on toast

Cheese on Toast

Use different kinds of cheese: Cheddar, Gruyere, Brie, Mozzarella, etc. Add things to go under the cheese, such as ham, pickle, Marmite, or sliced tomatoes. Slice or grate the cheese and place on top. Make sure the cheese covers the edges of the toast; it will protect the corners of the bread from being burned.

Tuna

Mix a can of tuna with 1 tablespoon mayo and season well with salt and pepper. Spread over the toasted bread and put grated Cheddar over the top. Grill until the cheese begins to brown.

Salmon

Mix a tin of salmon with 3 chopped spring onions. Spread over the toast. Mix 1 small pot of cottage cheese with 1 mug of grated cheddar cheese and spread over the salmon. Grill until the cheese begins to brown.

Beans on Toast with Egg on Top

Toast the bread, heat the beans, and then fry or poach the eggs (page 92). Great with HP sauce.

interesting sandwiches

One way to make sandwiches more interesting is to vary the bread you use. Try to avoid white bread all the time, as all the good stuff has been taken out and some not so good stuff added in! Choose different kinds of wholemeal or granary loaves, bread buns or pitta breads.

Beef with Cream Cheese and Sun-Dried Tomato

Mix a finely chopped, sun-dried tomato with about 150g cream cheese. Spread on one slice of bread and add the sliced beef and some lettuce.

Cottage Cheese & Banana

Spread the bread with a liberal amount of honey or jam and top with cottage cheese. Slice a banana and pile into the sandwich. Squash the other slice of bread on top to keep everything together.

Tuna & Hard-Boiled Egg

Drain a 185g tin of tuna. Put half in a bowl. Hard-boil 2 eggs (see video link below). Peel and chop and add to the bowl. Chop 2 spring onions and add to the bowl with 1 tablespoon of mayo. Mix together and season well.

Egg Mayo

Hard-boil 2 eggs (see video link below). Rinse them under cold water, take off the shells and chop them up with a knife. Mix them together with 1 tablespoon of mayo and season with salt and pepper.

Bacon & Banana

Grill or fry 3 slices of streaky bacon until crisp. Whilst it is still hot, put in the sandwich with a sliced banana. Squash the top slice on to keep everything in.

Chicken, Mayo & Lettuce

If you have roasted a chicken and have some spare, cut it into small pieces. Spread mayo over one slice of bread and add the lettuce. Season with salt and pepper. Add the chicken on top and place the other slice of bread on top.

Bacon & Brie

Grill or fry 3 slices of streaky bacon until crisp. Slice the Brie, add to the sandwich and serve whilst the bacon is still hot.

Smoked Salmon & Cream Cheese

Use the thin sandwich slices of smoked salmon. Spread one slice with cream cheese, add some sliced cucumber and a sliced spring onion, along with the smoked salmon.

Scrambled Eggs & Cheese and Tomato

Grate 1/2 mug cheese. Chop a tomato, quite finely. Heat a little butter in a small non-stick saucepan, add the tomatoes and fry for 1 minute. Add 2 beaten eggs and cook until they begin to set, stirring steadily. Take off the heat, add the cheese and stir. Season well and make the sandwich whilst the eggs are still hot.

Watch our boil an egg video
noshbooks.com/boil-an-egg

salads

These salads can be served with many of the recipes as an alternative to the ones suggested. They are also great to use with barbeques. Once you get into making salads, you can vary these to your taste and even begin to make up your own.

£0.35 /PERSON

£0.34 /PERSON

£0.43 /PERSON

Minty Potato Salad

4 medium **potatoes**, cut into small chunks, or 8 new potatoes

2 tablespoons **crème fraîche** or **soured cream**

3 tablespoons **Greek yogurt**

4 **spring onions**, chopped

2 tablespoons freshly chopped **mint** (or a teaspoon of dried mint)

salt and **pepper**

Cook the potatoes for 10 minutes. Leave to cool and then mix all the ingredients together.

Carrot and Apple Salad

1 large **carrot**

2 **red eating apples**

2 **spring onions**

6 **basil leaves**

juice of a **lemon**

2 tablespoons **olive oil**

salt and **pepper**

Put the carrots, apples, onions and basil through the coarse grater of the food processor. Alternatively, grate the carrot and apple and chop the onions and basil. Mix together with the oil and lemon juice and season well.

Rice Salad

³/₄ mug **rice** + 1 teaspoon **pilau seasoning**

1 **apple**, unpeeled, cored and chopped into chunks

2 sticks **celery**, chopped

2 tablespoons **raisins**

1 tablespoon **freshly chopped herbs**

1 mug **frozen peas**, defrosted

3 **spring onions**, chopped

3 tablespoons **mayo**

1 tablespoon **olive oil**

juice of a **lemon**

Cook the rice and add the peas to the pan 2 minutes before the end of the cooking time. Leave to cool. Mix the rest of the ingredients together.

£0.69 /PERSON

£0.62 /PERSON

£0.59 /PERSON

Green Salad with Croutons

2 slices **wholemeal bread**

1 tablespoon **olive oil**

1 **little gem lettuce**, sliced

2 **spring onions**, sliced

1 tablespoon **freshly chopped basil**

2 sticks **celery**, finely sliced

1 **green apple**, finely sliced

grated **Parmesan**

Heat the oil in a frying pan and add the bread. Fry on both sides until browned. Cut into small squares. Mix with the rest of the ingredients and sprinkle the Parmesan over the top.

Couscous Salad

1/2 mug **couscous**

4 **spring onions**, chopped

1 tablespoon **fresh parsley**, chopped

1 tablespoon **fresh basil**, chopped

1 tin of **sweetcorn**

1 **red pepper**, finely chopped

2 tablespoons **olive oil**

juice and rind of a **lemon**

1 teaspoon **sugar**

salt and **pepper**

Put the couscous in a bowl and add 1 mug of boiling water. Put a plate over and leave to stand for 4 minutes. Leave to cool slightly and add the rest of the ingredients. Mix together.

Celery, Fennel and Apple Salad

2 **little gem lettuces**, finely sliced

4 **spring onions**, chopped

1/2 **fennel bulb**, finely sliced

1 **red apple**, cored and finely sliced

2 sticks **celery**, finely sliced

8cm piece **cucumber**, cut into thin strips

Dressing

salt and **pepper**

2 tablespoons **olive oil**

juice of a **lemon**

1 teaspoon **sugar**

Mix the salad ingredients together. Mix the dressing together, pour over and distribute well.

lunch boxes

Lunch boxes don't need to be a chore, or have the same old things in every day. You will be bored and the kids will also be bored. Ask your children what others have in their lunch boxes and you may find some ideas you want to copy. Most lunch boxes will contain a sandwich, fruit, drink and a chocolate/fruity bar, but there are variations to be made on this theme.

Sandwiches

If you find that you get the crusts back every day, then just cut them off in the first place. If you have the patience, cut the sandwiches into shapes. The fillings can be quite simple: ham, chicken, tuna, etc. Salad will have gone soggy by lunchtime and, if you give them eggs, other kids will complain about the smell! Put a few carrot or cucumber sticks, tiny cheese cubes or cherry tomatoes with the sandwiches.

Fruit is Great

Apples, bananas, grapes and peeled satsumas work well. Some children like dried fruit, such as raisins or apricots. An alternative to this is to put some fruit in jelly and give them a portion each day - either fresh strawberries etc, or use packets of preserved fruit, or tinned fruit. Tinned fruit is better than no fruit. Choose the jelly without sugar added. The jelly and fruit will last about 3 days.

Yogurt

You can buy the small pots, but a cheaper way is to have a small clip top box (easy for them to open) with natural yogurt and a few pieces of frozen fruit, plus some honey in it (see photo opposite). Come lunch-time the fruit will be defrosted and they can give it a stir.

Fruit Bars/Cakes

You can freeze "Fruit Muffins" (see page 226), or "Apricot Flap Jacks" (page 223) and just bring out enough for each day. They will be thawed by lunchtime, but also serve to keep the rest of the lunchbox cool.

Drinks

Boxed drinks are the easiest, or you can buy an easily-sealed drink bottle and fill it each day.

Another idea is to make Friday a treat day, so the lunch box may include a chocolate bar, or a bag of crisps.

pastry

If you have never made pastry before, here is an easy recipe for shortcrust pastry. I never seem to have the time to make puff pastry and always buy that ready-made. Shortcrust, however, is simple when you know how and here is the 'know how'!

175g **butter,** cold from the fridge (measure using packet)

2 mugs/340g **self-raising flour**

1 beaten **egg**

¼ mug **water**

1 Cut the butter into small pieces and add the flour.

2 Rub in the butter and flour using your fingers and thumbs. Don't use the palms of your hands, as they will be warm. Keep going until the mixture resembles breadcrumbs. Alternatively, place in a food-proccessor, or food-mixer, on slowish speed and let it do the work for you. Either way, don't overmix.

3 Add sufficient egg and water to make a soft dough. Turn out onto a floured board and squash together. Handle as little as possible; don't knead the dough, save that for bread.

4 Pop in the fridge for about 30 minutes.

5 Turn back onto the floured board and roll out with even movements. Keep turning the dough, so that the edges stay the same thickness as the middle.

6 Pull the pastry back over the rolling-pin and place on the casserole or flan dish.

Pastry is usually baked at 180ºC fan oven/200ºc/gas 6, but this may change according to the contents of the dish.

MENU 1

MONDAY
BACON AND MOZZARELLA PASTA BAKE - P69

TUESDAY
BEEF AND POTATO HOT POT - P72

WEDNESDAY
SUPER SIMPLE TUNA BAKE - P171

THURSDAY
ONE-POT CHICKEN HOT POT - P188

FRIDAY
PASTITSIO - P204

SATURDAY
EGG-FRIED PLOUGHMAN'S - P94 (LUNCH)
SPICED CHICKEN AND HERB COUSCOUS - P154 (DINNER)

SUNDAY
SLOW-COOK ROAST PORK - P120

SHOPPING LIST

- [ ] 13 Medium potatoes
- [ ] 2 sweet potatoes
- [ ] 15 tomatoes
- [ ] 4 onions
- [ ] 1 yellow pepper
- [ ] 1 red onion
- [ ] green veg for 1 meal
- [ ] 1 eating apple
- [ ] 10 carrots
- [ ] 1 piece broccoli
- [ ] bunch spring onions
- [ ] 2 lemons
- [ ] garlic
- [ ] fresh basil
- [ ] fresh coriander
- [ ] 300g smoked streaky bacon
- [ ] 750g beef mince
- [ ] 500g beef mince
- [ ] 8 boneless chicken thighs
- [ ] 3 chicken breasts
- [ ] 1kg piece pork shoulder
- [ ] 1kg Cheddar cheese
- [ ] 300ml double cream
- [ ] 300ml soured cream
- [ ] 200g feta cheese
- [ ] 2 balls mozzarella
- [ ] 4 eggs
- [ ] frozen peas
- [ ] sun-dried tomatoes

- [ ] 2 small packets crisps
- [ ] tin baked beans
- [ ] tin chopped tomatoes
- [ ] 2 tins tuna
- [ ] 1 wholemeal loaf

Check cupboards
- [ ] pasta (3 meals)
- [ ] oil
- [ ] stock cubes
- [ ] tomato purée
- [ ] Worcestershire sauce
- [ ] salt and pepper
- [ ] butter
- [ ] dried basil
- [ ] flour
- [ ] mixed herbs
- [ ] HP sauce
- [ ] pickle
- [ ] cumin
- [ ] ground coriander
- [ ] paprika
- [ ] couscous
- [ ] fennel seeds

MENU 2

MONDAY
HONEY CHICKEN BAKE - P64

TUESDAY
GINGER CHICKEN STIR-FRY - P76

WEDNESDAY
BALSAMIC CHILLI BEEF RAGU - P84

THURSDAY
BANGERS AND SWEET POTATO MASH - P136

FRIDAY
CHORIZO AND PANCETTA BAKE - P70

SATURDAY
GRILLED TUNA BAGELS - P40 (LUNCH)

MOROCCAN LAMB PIE - P100 (DINNER)

SUNDAY
CREAMY PORK AND MUSHROOM STEW - P112

SHOPPING LIST

- [ ] Savoy cabbage
- [ ] 10 potatoes
- [ ] celery
- [ ] 10 carrots
- [ ] piece of fresh ginger (for 2 meals)
- [ ] 7 onions
- [ ] 2 courgettes
- [ ] 19 mushrooms
- [ ] 4 tomatoes
- [ ] 1 lemon
- [ ] 2 bunches spring onions
- [ ] 2 sweet potatoes
- [ ] 2 fat red chillies
- [ ] 1 red pepper
- [ ] 2 yellow pepper
- [ ] 1 broccoli
- [ ] fresh coriander
- [ ] fresh basil
- [ ] fresh parsley
- [ ] 6 chicken breasts
- [ ] 750g stewing pork
- [ ] 500g lamb mince
- [ ] 500g beef mince
- [ ] 100g pack pancetta lardons
- [ ] 8 large sausages
- [ ] pkt streaky bacon
- [ ] 4 small chorizo sausages
- [ ] 400g pack fresh or straight-to-wok egg noodles
- [ ] 750g Cheddar cheese
- [ ] 300 ml double cream
- [ ] small piece of Parmesan
- [ ] 8 eggs
- [ ] 4 bagels
- [ ] 2 tins tuna
- [ ] 3 tins tomatoes
- [ ] baked beans
- [ ] small wholemeal loaf

Check cupboards
- [ ] flour
- [ ] paprika
- [ ] mixed herbs
- [ ] dried thyme
- [ ] ground coriander
- [ ] cumin
- [ ] golden syrup
- [ ] oil
- [ ] butter
- [ ] stock cubes
- [ ] tomato purée
- [ ] bread
- [ ] mayo
- [ ] honey
- [ ] soy
- [ ] garlic (6 cloves)
- [ ] olives
- [ ] white wine vinegar
- [ ] toasted sesame oil
- [ ] balsamic vinegar
- [ ] Worcestershire Sauce
- [ ] penne pasta

MENU 3

MONDAY
SAUSAGE AND VEG TRAYBAKE – P196

TUESDAY
ONE-POT CHICKEN KORMA – P82

WEDNESDAY
CRUNCHY TOPPED TUNA BAKE – P86

THURSDAY
BEEF AND MUSHROOM CASSEROLE – P124

FRIDAY
SMOKED SALMON AND CREAM CHEESE SPAGHETTI – P193

SATURDAY
HONEY, CARROT AND LEEK SOUP – P43 (LUNCH)

CHICKEN QUESADILLAS – P176 (DINNER)

SUNDAY
CHICKEN AND LEEK PIE – P130

SHOPPING LIST

- [ ] 8 potatoes
- [ ] 5 onions
- [ ] 1 red onion
- [ ] 2 parsnips
- [ ] 2 sweet potatoes
- [ ] 6 tomatoes
- [ ] 200g fresh spinach
- [ ] 1kg mushrooms
- [ ] 125g cherry tomatoes
- [ ] green salad (one meal)
- [ ] 2 courgettes
- [ ] bunch spring onions
- [ ] 2 lemons
- [ ] fresh basil
- [ ] 5 leeks
- [ ] 8 carrots
- [ ] 10 large sausages
- [ ] 8 chicken breasts
- [ ] 750g stewing beef
- [ ] 200g smoked salmon trimmings
- [ ] 2 eggs
- [ ] 300g cream cheese with garlic and herbs
- [ ] streaky bacon
- [ ] 750g Cheddar cheese
- [ ] 100g pine nuts
- [ ] 300ml double cream
- [ ] small carton natural yogurt

- [ ] small wholemeal loaf
- [ ] bread for cheese on toast
- [ ] 2 tins tuna
- [ ] corn tortillas
- [ ] tin tomatoes

Check cupboards
- [ ] butter
- [ ] oil
- [ ] flour
- [ ] honey
- [ ] rosemary
- [ ] paprika
- [ ] bay leaf
- [ ] tomato purée
- [ ] white wine vinegar
- [ ] stock cubes
- [ ] garlic (3 cloves)
- [ ] Korma curry paste
- [ ] rice
- [ ] raisins
- [ ] pasta (1 meal)
- [ ] spaghetti
- [ ] milk
- [ ] pickle

MENU 4

MONDAY
CREAMY CHICKEN AND MUSHROOM PIE - P60

TUESDAY
HOISIN AND SESAME TUNA NOODLES - P52

WEDNESDAY
ONE-POT BEEF COBBLER - P122

THURSDAY
SPICED APRICOT TURKEY BURGERS - P166

FRIDAY
CORNED BEEF HASH WITH POACHED EGGS - P190

SATURDAY
SIMPLE SATURDAY BRUNCH - P90 (LUNCH)

CHICKEN NUGGETS AND WEDGES - P180 (DINNER)

SUNDAY
SCRUMPY PORK PIE - P106

SHOPPING LIST

- ☐ 1 large sweet potato
- ☐ 20 potatoes
- ☐ green veg for Sunday
- ☐ celery
- ☐ 5 onions
- ☐ broccoli
- ☐ yellow pepper
- ☐ 4 carrots
- ☐ 2 bunches spring onions
- ☐ 20 mushrooms
- ☐ 4 tomatoes
- ☐ fresh parsley
- ☐ fresh basil
- ☐ 300g ready-to-wok or fresh, egg noodles
- ☐ 4 sausages
- ☐ 450g turkey breast
- ☐ 6 chicken breasts
- ☐ 500g beef mince
- ☐ 500g pork mince
- ☐ 8 rashers bacon
- ☐ 12 eggs
- ☐ frozen peas
- ☐ 200g Cheddar cheese
- ☐ 300g cream cheese with garlic and herbs
- ☐ 300ml double cream
- ☐ suet
- ☐ 350g tin corned beef
- ☐ 2 tins tuna
- ☐ tin baked beans

- ☐ 4 burger buns
- ☐ wholemeal loaf
- ☐ ½ pint cider
- ☐ 1 sheet puff pastry
- ☐ hoisin sauce

Check cupboards
- ☐ tomato sauce
- ☐ butter
- ☐ flour
- ☐ oil
- ☐ garlic (4 cloves)
- ☐ stock cubes
- ☐ sesame oil
- ☐ soy sauce
- ☐ honey
- ☐ dried coriander
- ☐ cumin
- ☐ dried mixed herbs
- ☐ basil
- ☐ thyme
- ☐ paprika
- ☐ ready-to-eat apricots

quick bites

Saturday lunch-time, kids home from school, or on school holidays, not much time, but everyone hungry? Here are a few inexpensive and quick ideas to feed the hungry hordes. Some of these recipes you can freeze beforehand, to be prepared for those busy days.

Grilled Tuna Bagels

4 **bagels**, cut in half horizontally

2 x 200g tin of **tuna**, drained

2 tablespoons **mayo**

juice of ½ **lemon**

8 **spring onions**, chopped

2 mugs grated **cheese**

1 Lightly toast the bagels.

2 Mix the tuna, mayo, lemon juice and onions together. Place on the bottom half of the bagels and sprinkle with the grated cheese.

3 Place under a hot grill until the cheese melts.

Ham and Cheese Pinwheels

375g pack of **ready-rolled puff pastry**

3 slices of thick **ham**, or quite a few slices of the wafer-thin stuff.

1 mug grated **cheese**

2 **spring onions**, chopped

1 beaten **egg**

1   Preheat the oven to 200ºC fan oven/220ºC/gas 7. Grease a large baking tray.

2   Unroll the pastry sheet and place the sliced ham over the pastry. Sprinkle the cheese and onion evenly over the ham. Season with salt and pepper (You can make this recipe using chopped, uncooked bacon and half a chopped onion, instead of the ham and spring onions. This will give a stronger taste).

3   Roll up lengthways into a 'long sausage' and cut into 1cm slices. Lay them flat on the baking tray.

4   Brush the tops with the beaten egg and place in the oven for 15 minutes, or until browned.

Sweet Potato and Lentil Soup

2 tablespoons **oil**

2 **red onions**, sliced

3 cloves of **garlic**, chopped

4 medium **sweet potatoes**, peeled and cut into 3cm chunks

1 dessertspoon mild **curry paste (GF option)**

4 mugs **water**

½ mug **red lentils**

1 **vegetable stock cube/pot (GF option)**

1 eating **apple**, cored, peeled and chopped roughly

juice of a **lemon**

1 tablespoon freshly chopped **coriander**, or 1 teaspoon **dried coriander**

salt and **pepper**

1 Heat the oil in a large saucepan and add the onions, garlic and sweet potatoes. Fry until they begin to soften.

2 Add the curry paste, water, lentils, stock and apple. Bring to the boil, then turn down to simmer for 20 minutes.

3 Blend with a hand-held blender until smooth. Add the lemon juice, salt and pepper and coriander. Stir. If the soup is really thick, add a little more water.

Honey, Carrot and Leek Soup

75g **butter** (measure on packet)

3 small **leeks**, sliced

8 large **carrots**, roughly chopped

3 teaspoons clear **honey**

½ teaspoon **paprika**

2 **bay leaves**

2 **vegetable stock cubes/pots (GF option)**

4 mugs **water**

Cheese on Toast

bread (GF option)

Cheddar cheese

sweet pickle

1. Melt the butter in a large saucepan over a medium heat. Add the leeks to the pan and fry for 2–3 minutes until they begin to soften.

2. Add the carrots, honey, paprika and bay leaves. Cook for 2 minutes.

3. Pour in the water and the stock. Bring to the boil and then simmer for 25 minutes. Take out the bay leaves, blend the soup and season to taste. Serve with cheese on toast, cut into 'soldiers'.

£0.54 /PERSON | SERVES 4 | EASE ★★★☆☆ | PREP 10 MINS | COOK 30 MINS | V GF OPTION

Roasted Sweet Potato Soup

NOTE: This is ideal for using up the leftover veggies that lurk in the fridge at the end of the week. Cooking double and freezing for another day makes sense too.

ONE MORE THING: To blend your soup, it is best if you have a hand-held blender, or you could use a food processor.

1 large **sweet potato**, peeled and cut into 3cm chunks

2 **carrots**, peeled and cut into strips

6 **tomatoes**, cut in half

1 **onion**, cut into wedges

2 tablespoons **olive oil**

1 sprig **fresh rosemary** leaves, or 1 teaspoon **dried rosemary**

3½-4 mugs boiling **water**

1 vegetable **stock pot/cube (GF option)**

serve with **croutons** (see page 29) (GF option)

1 Preheat the oven to 200ºC fan oven/220ºC/gas 7.

2 Put the vegetables on a large roasting tin or baking tray. Sprinkle with the oil and rosemary. Season well and mix everything up with your hands, leaving the tomatoes face up. Spread everything evenly on the tray. Put in the oven for 30 minutes.

3 Once the vegetables are nicely browned, tip them and their juices into a saucepan, with 3½ mugs of water and the stock. Blitz, but not too much.

4 Bring to the boil. Add the other ½ mug of water, if necessary. The soup should be quite thick and not watery. Take off the heat and taste for seasoning. Serve with some crusty bread, or croutons (see page 29).

£0.85 /PERSON · SERVES 4 · EASE ★★☆☆☆ · PREP 20 MINS · COOK 10 MINS · OK TO FREEZE ❄ · V GF OPTION

Sun-Dried Tomato Soup with Parmesan Toast

NOTE: You can replace the Parmesan with Cheddar if you have long since given up the battle to introduce Parmesan to your kids.

WHERE ON EARTH: Sun-dried tomatoes can be found next to the pickles and olives, etc.

25g **butter** (measure using packet)

2 **red onions**, chopped

3 **celery** sticks, sliced

2 cloves **garlic**, chopped

425g cans **butter beans**, washed and drained

1/2 x 290g jar of **sun-dried tomatoes**, chopped

3 mugs **water**

2 **vegetable stock pots/ cubes (GF option)**

1 teaspoon freshly-chopped **rosemary** leaves or 1/2 teaspoon **dried rosemary**

Parmesan Toast

6 slices **wholemeal bread (GF option)**

butter

1 mug grated **Parmesan**

1 Heat the butter in a large saucepan. Add the onions and celery and fry until they begin to brown.

2 Add the rest of the soup ingredients and bring to the boil. Season well and simmer for 10 minutes.

3 Meanwhile, lightly toast the bread. Butter it and put the grated Parmesan on the top. Place under the grill until the cheese begins to bubble.

4 Once the soup is cooked, blitz with a hand-held blender, or put in the food-processor. It does not need to be really smooth; leave it a bit rustic.

PETER & BERNICE: "My family HATE butter beans, but they loved this soup. I love that it includes a cheap vegetarian source of protein in an innovative way. The strong flavour of the sun-dried tomatoes makes this soup much more exciting than a regular tomato soup. It tastes creamy without adding any cream! Crispy Parmesan toast contrasts beautifully with the smooth soup."

Spicy Butternut Squash Soup

1 tablespoon **olive oil**

1 **onion**, sliced

1kg **butternut squash**, peeled and cut into chunks

½ mug **red lentils**

3 mugs **water**

2 **stock pots/cubes (GF option)**

1 dessertspoon **Korma curry paste (GF option)** (optional)

1 Heat the oil in a large saucepan and fry the onions and squash until they begin to brown.

2 Add the lentils, water, stock and curry paste. Season well and bring to the boil. Turn down to simmer for 15 minutes. The squash and the lentils should be tender by then.

3 Blitz with a hand-held blender, or food processor.

4 Serve with some crusty bread and cheese.

Mozzarella Stuffed Tomatoes

4 **beef tomatoes** (or large ones)

125g **mozzarella cheese**, chopped up

1 tablespoon freshly chopped **basil**

2 pieces of **ready-roasted red peppers**, roughly chopped

1 tablespoon **red pesto**

4 slices of **crusty bread (GF option)**

1 Preheat the oven to 180ºC fan oven/200ºC/gas 6. Grease a baking tray.

2 Cut the top off the tomatoes and keep for later. Scoop out the fleshy middles of the tomatoes with a spoon (you can save them for spag bol later).

3 Mix the cheese, basil, peppers and pesto together and pile it into the tomatoes. Put the tops back on and place on the greased tray.

4 Place in the oven for 20 minutes.

5 Meanwhile, toast and butter the bread.

6 Once the tomatoes are cooked, place one on each slice of bread and pour over any juice which may have escaped.

Mushroom Omelette with Apple and Fennel Salad

NOTE: You can replace the mushrooms with things like tomatoes, small roast potatoes, ham, tuna, prawns, etc. This recipe just gives the basic idea for an omelette.

1 tablespoon **olive oil**

6 **eggs**, beaten

300g pack of **button mushrooms**, sliced

6 **spring onions**, chopped

1 tablespoon freshly chopped **basil**

¼ mug **water**

²/₃ mug **cheese**

Salad

1 **little gem lettuce**, finely sliced

3 **spring onions**, chopped

½ **fennel** bulb, finely sliced

1 **red apple**, cored and finely sliced

2 sticks **celery**, finely sliced

8cm piece **cucumber**, cut into thin strips

Dressing

salt and **pepper**

2 tablespoons **olive oil**

juice of a **lemon**

1 teaspoon **sugar**

1 Prepare the salad by mixing the ingredients in a bowl. Mix the dressing ingredients and pour over. Use a couple of forks to distribute well.

2 Put the grill on a high heat.

3 Heat the oil in a large frying pan. Add the mushrooms and spring onions and fry on a high heat, until the mushrooms begin to brown. Season well with salt and pepper.

4 Mix together the water, basil and eggs and beat. Pour into the frying pan. Allow the egg mixture on the bottom of the pan to set, then gently push around to allow the unset mixture to get to the bottom of the pan. Do this one more time.

5 While there is still a little runny egg in the pan, sprinkle the cheese evenly over the top.

6 Place under the hot grill for 3–4 minutes, until the cheese bubbles and browns. Serve with the salad.

Watch a video of making omelettes at
noshbooks.com/omelette

Hoisin and Sesame Tuna Noodles

NOTE: This is essentially a "one-pot" dish too, so not too heavy on the washing up.

2 tablespoons **sesame oil**, to fry

8 **spring onions**, chopped

1 clove **garlic**, finely chopped

6 **mushrooms**, sliced

4 medium **tomatoes**, cut into 1/8's

2 tablespoons **soy**

1 tablespoon **honey**

1/2 mug **water**

1 tablespoon **hoisin sauce**

2 x 150g pack of **ready-to-wok noodles or fresh noodles**

2 tins **tuna**, drained

1 Heat the sesame oil in a wok and fry the onions and garlic for 30 seconds.

2 Add the mushrooms and tomatoes and fry for a further 30 seconds.

3 Mix together the soy, honey, water and hoisin. Add to the wok. Cook for 30 seconds.

4 Add the noodles and tuna and heat through for no more than 30 seconds. Stir as little as possible, so the tuna does not go mushy.

BEN & NICOLE: "Ridiculously simple. I didn't know I could cook a whole meal in such a short space of time."

everyday fast food

You come home from work, or at the end of a busy day looking after the children and you want something uncomplicated. You also don't want the same old thing over and over again. Some of these recipes take minutes to prepare and then cook in the oven for a while. All in all, they won't take much of your precious time.

Apple and Coconut Sweet Curry

NOTE: This is a lovely, mild, sweet curry, ideal for younger children who don't want too much spice. You can up the quantity of curry paste, or use hotter curry paste, such as Madras, if you prefer a stronger taste.

oil to fry

1 **onion**, chopped

3 **chicken breasts**, cut into bite-sized pieces

2 tablespoons **Korma curry paste (GF option)**

1 tin **coconut milk**

1 **chicken stock pot/cube (GF option)**

8 **mushrooms**, sliced

2 large **tomatoes**, chopped

1 **red apple**, cut into small chunks

1/2 mug **raisins**

rice to serve (see page 16)

1 Put the rice on to cook (see page 16).

2 Heat a little oil in a wok. Add the onions and fry until they begin to soften. Add the chicken and cook until no longer pink. Add the Korma paste and cook for 30 seconds.

3 Add the coconut milk and stock.

4 Add the mushrooms, tomatoes, apple and raisins and cook for 1 minute. Bring to the boil, then turn down to simmer for 5–6 minutes. Season with salt and pepper.

5 Serve together with the cooked rice.

GARY & NIKKI: "My kids don't usually like curry, but they liked this one."

Watch a video of how to make perfect rice at
noshbooks.com/rice

Moroccan Honey Chicken

NOTE: Depending on your family, or your own taste, you can add the juice of half the lemon to the couscous, along with the rind, if you want to add a little extra kick.

1 mug **couscous**

grated rind of a **lemon**

2 mugs boiling **water**

1 **chicken stock pot/cube**

1 tablespoon **oil**

1 **onion**, sliced

1 **red pepper,** cut into small chunks

1 clove **garlic**, finely chopped

3 **chicken breasts**, cut into bite-sized pieces

400g tin **chickpeas**, washed and drained

1 teaspoon **cumin**

1 teaspoon **coriander**

1½ tablespoons **honey**

1 teaspoon **cinnamon**

¼ teaspoon **chilli** powder (optional)

400g tin **chopped tomatoes**

1 Put the couscous in a bowl with the lemon rind. Add the boiling water and the stock. Stir once. Put a plate over the bowl and leave to absorb all of the water. This should take 4–5 minutes.

2 Heat the oil in a large saucepan or wok. Add the onions, garlic and peppers and fry until they begin to soften.

3 Add the chicken and season with salt and pepper. Cook until the chicken is no longer pink.

4 Add the rest of the ingredients (excluding the couscous) and bring to the boil. Turn down to simmer for 5–6 minutes.

5 Serve as seen in the photo opposite.

Creamy Chicken and Mushroom Pie

NOTE: If your shallow casserole dish does not have a lid, just use some foil.

ONE MORE THING: A great way to do your carrots is to bake them in the oven in a covered dish. Do this before you start preparing your chicken pie, so they should be ready by the time your pie is finished. Just bake them with a little water, butter, salt and pepper. You can even drizzle over some honey, just before serving, to make them even tastier.

4 large **potatoes**, cut into 2cm cubes

50g **butter,** measured using packet

300g pack of **Philadelphia cream cheese with garlic & herbs**

300ml carton **double cream**

chicken stock pot/cube (GF option)

3 **chicken breasts,** cut into bite-sized pieces

6 **spring onions**, chopped

8 **mushrooms,** sliced

1 mug defrosted **frozen peas**

6–8 medium **carrots,** sliced

1 Preheat the oven to 180ºC fan oven/200ºC/gas 6. Grease a large, shallow, casserole dish with oil.

2 Heat water to boiling in a saucepan, add the cubed potatoes and season with salt. Bring back to the boil, then turn down to simmer for 10 minutes. Drain and add the butter, allowing it to melt. Put a lid on the pan and shake the potatoes to distribute the butter evenly.

3 Mix the cream cheese and the cream together in a bowl until smooth. Add the chicken stock and season with salt and pepper.

4 Add the chicken, onions, mushrooms and peas into a shallow casserole dish and mix together. Pour into a casserole dish

5 Pour the creamy mix over the top.

6 Put the potatoes on top. Place in the oven for 20 minutes with a lid on and for a further 25-30 minutes with the lid off, until the potatoes are browned.

7 Serve with boiled carrots.

BEN & NICOLE: "Bella loved this, Toby did eat some, but he is being generally picky at the moment."

Fennel Chicken Pasta

NOTE: Some younger children may find the taste of the fennel seeds a bit strange. You could just leave them out, as there are plenty of other tasty ingredients.

250g **tagliatelli or spaghetti (GF option)**

3 **chicken breasts**

1/2 teaspoon **fennel seeds**

100g pack **pine nuts**

1 tablespoon **oil**

1 **red onion**, chopped

1 **clove** garlic, finely chopped

5 **tomatoes**, chopped

5 **sun-dried tomatoes**, chopped

juice of a **lemon**

1 teaspoon **sugar**

1 Cook the pasta (see page 17), drain and set to one side.

2 Half fill a medium pan with boiling water, put the 3 chicken breasts in the water and bring back to the boil. Turn the heat off, put a lid on the pan and leave for 15 minutes. After that time, choose the largest piece and check that it is cooked through. If not, bring back to the boil again and leave to stand for 5 minutes. Cut into bite-sized pieces.

3 Put the pine nuts and fennel seeds in a dry frying pan and toast for about 1 minute, until the pine nuts begin to brown. Shake the pan to move the nuts around. Take out of the pan and leave until needed.

4 Heat the oil in the frying pan and fry the onions and garlic until the onions become soft. Add the tomatoes and the sun-dried tomatoes and fry for 2-3 minutes until the tomatoes begin to lose their shape. Add the lemon juice, nuts, fennel seeds and the sugar and heat through. Season well.

5 Add the chicken to the tomato mixture and spoon over the pasta. Serve.

JOE & SARAH: "Nice and light, good for the summer and easy too."

Honey Chicken Bake

NOTE: If you ever have some dry bread that you would normally throw away, why not make it into breadcrumbs and put it in the freezer for a later date.

3 **chicken breasts,** cut into bite-sized pieces

1½ tablespoons **honey**

1½ tablespoons **soy (GF option)**

oil to fry

2 **onions**, sliced

1 clove **garlic**, finely chopped

2 medium **courgettes**, cut into small pieces

6 **mushrooms**, sliced

1 teaspoon dried **mixed herbs** or 1 tablespoon fresh mixed herbs

4 **tomatoes**, chopped

12 **olives**, halved (optional)

4 slices **bread (GF option)**, made into breadcrumbs

1 mug grated **cheese**

1 Grease a large casserole dish with oil.

2 Put the chicken in a bowl and add the honey and soy. Mix together and leave until needed.

3 Heat a little oil in a frying pan and fry the onions and garlic until they begin to soften. Add the courgettes, mushrooms and mixed herbs. Fry on a medium heat for 5 minutes.

4 Add the chicken and the juices and cook for 2–3 minutes

5 Add the tomatoes and olives and season well. Cook on a high heat for 2 minutes. Pour everything into the casserole dish.

6 Mix the breadcrumbs and cheese together and sprinkle evenly over the casserole dish.

7 Place under grill for 5–10 minutes until the cheese is browned.

ADAM & CONNIE: "Very appealing, full of flavour and fairly cheap to make. Really good way of getting vegetables into the kids".

EASE ★★★☆☆ PREP 30 MINS COOK 35 MINS OK TO FREEZE

£ 1.47 /PERSON SERVES 6

Chicken and Roast Vegetable Couscous

NOTE: Any leftovers here can be frozen and used for lunch boxes, as it doesn't need to be hot to be yummy. You can also serve this cold with salad.

2 large **sweet potatoes**, peeled and cut into 2cm cubes

2 **courgettes**, cut into small pieces

4 large **tomatoes**, roughly chopped

6 **mushrooms**, sliced

2 **onions**, chopped

1 teaspoon **cumin**

1 teaspoon ground **coriander**

1 teaspoon ground **cinnamon**

4 tablespoons **olive oil**

1 mug **couscous**

2 mugs boiling **water**

2 **chicken stock pots/cubes**

2 tablespoons **sun-dried tomato purée** (can use normal tomato purée)

oil to fry

3 **chicken breasts**

1 Preheat the oven to 200ºC fan oven/220ºC/ gas 7.

2 Place all the vegetables on a large baking tray with the spices and the oil. Use your hands to spread everything evenly. Season with salt and pepper. Cook in the oven for 30–35 minutes until the vegetables are browned.

3 Place the couscous in a large bowl and add the water, chicken stock and tomato puree. Stir well. Cover and leave until needed.

4 Heat a little oil in a frying pan and pan roast the chicken breast. Cook on a high heat for 2 minutes each side. Turn down the heat, cover the pan with a lid or foil and cook for 4 minutes each side. Cut or tear into small pieces and add on top of the couscous.

5 Mix the cooked vegetables and any juices to the couscous and serve.

BEN & NICOLE: "This is one of our favourite easy-to-cook meals."

Watch a video of pan roasting chicken at
noshbooks.com/pan-chicken

Coconut Poached Thai Chicken

LEE & SARAH: "Good basis for a family to try, not being too hot and able to add more zing next time you cook it. This was a real hit with all. Yum!"

1 **chicken stock pot/ cube (GF option)**

1 tablespoon grated fresh **ginger** (2cm diameter)

3 **chicken breasts**, cut into bite-sized pieces

1 tablespoon **Thai red curry paste (GF option)** (add extra if your kids are happy with spice)

400ml can **coconut milk**

6 **spring onions**, chopped

1 tablespoon **fish sauce**

6 **mushrooms**, sliced

juice of a **lime**

1 dessertspoon **cornflour** mixed with a little water

2 tablespoons freshly chopped **coriander**

1½ mugs **basmati rice**

1 Cook the rice (see page 16).

2 Put everything but the fresh coriander and cornflour into a saucepan or wok and bring to the boil. Simmer gently for 10 minutes.

3 Add the cornflour and stir until the sauce thickens. Stir in the coriander and serve with rice.

Bacon and Mozzarella Pasta Bake

a little **oil**

2 mugs **pasta (GF option)**

300g pack **smoked, streaky bacon**

6 medium-sized **tomatoes**, roughly chopped

4 large pieces of **sun-dried tomatoes**, chopped

1 tablespoon freshly chopped **basil**

300ml **double cream**

2 x 125g balls of **mozzarella**

1 slice **wholemeal bread (GF option)**, made into breadcrumbs

1 Preheat the oven to 180ºC fan oven/200ºC/gas 6. Grease a large casserole dish.

2 Cook the pasta, drain and leave until needed.

3 Fry the bacon until it is crispy and then chop into small pieces (kitchen scissors make this job easier).

4 Mix the bacon, sun-dried tomatoes, tomatoes and cream into the pasta and mix well. Season with pepper (the bacon will have enough salt). Pour into the casserole dish.

5 Pull apart the mozzarella and place over the pasta mix. Sprinkle the breadcrumbs over the top and place in the oven for 25 minutes until the cheese begins to brown.

6 Sprinkle the chopped basil over the top.

£ 1.39 /PERSON   SERVES 4   EASE ★★★☆☆   PREP 25 MINS   COOK 30 MINS

Chorizo and Pancetta Bake

NOTE: This is a complete meal in one dish. Really easy to do and lots of different textures and flavours to makes it unusual and interesting.

WHERE ON EARTH: Pancetta lardons can be found next to the cooked meats in the supermarket. Make sure you get pancetta lardons and not normal bacon lardons.

2 tablespoons **olive oil**

100g packet **pancetta lardons**

4 small **chorizo sausages**, sliced

1 **onion**, sliced

¼ mug **water**

6 **mushrooms**, sliced

2 **garlic** cloves, finely chopped

1 **red** or **yellow pepper**, chopped

400g tin chopped **tomatoes**

1 tablespoon **tomato purée**

3 tablespoons **fresh parsley**, chopped

6–8 large **eggs**

2 slices wholemeal **bread**, buttered and cut into small squares

1 Preheat the oven to 180ºC fan oven/200ºC/ gas 6. Grease a large casserole dish.

2 Heat a little oil in a wok and fry the pancetta and chorizo until they begin to brown. Take out and set to one side.

3 Add the onions, peppers and garlic to the pan and fry until they begin to brown.

4 Add the water, mushrooms, tomato purée and the tinned tomatoes. Simmer for 5–6 minutes.

5 Return the pancetta and chorizo to the pan and add the parsley. Stir in.

6 Pour into the casserole dish. Make small hollows in the mixture and break the eggs into each. Sprinkle the cubed bread over the top and place in the oven for 25–30 minutes. The eggs should be cooked and the bread crisp.

£1.25 /PERSON SERVES 4 | EASE ★★★☆☆ | PREP 25 MINS | COOK 55 MINS | OK TO FREEZE ❄

Beef and Potato Hot-Pot

NOTE: This is similar to our "Monday Pie" from "Nosh for Students", but we have included it in this book, as it is just perfect for families too.

ONE MORE THING: If you have a hob-to-oven casserole dish, this is a great one-pot dish. Easy to prepare and then just leave it in the oven to do its thing.

ACTUALLY...ONE MORE THING: You can use a food processor to slice the potatoes, it saves time and makes them nice and thin.

1 tablespoon **oil**, to fry

1 **onion**, sliced

750g pack of **beef mince**

1 **beef stock pot/cube**

1/2 mug water

400g tin **baked beans**

4 **tomatoes**, chopped

1 tablespoon **tomato purée**

1 tablespoon **Worcestershire sauce**

5 large **potatoes** (no need to peel), cut into 1/2 cm slices

green veg to serve

1 Preheat the oven to 180ºC fan oven/200ºC/gas 6.

2 Heat a little oil in a hob-to-oven casserole, or wok, and fry the onion until it becomes soft.

3 Add the mince and fry until no longer pink.

4 Add the stock, beans, tomatoes, tomato purée and Worcestershire sauce. Heat through and season well. Leave in the hob-to-oven casserole or transfer to a large, greased casserole dish.

5 Arrange the sliced potatoes evenly over the top of the meat mixture. Season well with salt and pepper.

6 Put the lid on the casserole and place in the oven for 30 minutes. Take the lid off and cook for a further 25 minutes. The potatoes should be browned.

7 Serve with green veg.

Lemon Couscous Salad

NOTE: Good one to freeze in portions for lunch boxes. If you take them out in the morning, they will be defrosted by lunch-time.

ONE MORE THING: This works best with fresh herbs. Try not to use freeze-dried ones.

1½ mugs **couscous**

3 mugs **water**

1 **chicken stock pot/cube**

oil to fry

1 **onion**, chopped

2 **courgettes**, chopped small

3 **chicken breasts**, cut into bite-sized chunks

6 **mushrooms**, sliced

3 **tomatoes**, chopped

12-16 **black olives**

Dressing

4 tablespoons **olive oil**

juice and grated rind of a **lemon**

1 tablespoon fresh **coriander**, chopped

1 tablespoon fresh **basil**, chopped

salt and **pepper**

¼ teaspoon **cumin**

¼ teaspoon **cayenne pepper**

1 Place the couscous in a bowl and add 3 mugs of boiling water and the stock. Cover with a plate and leave to stand for 5 minutes until all the water is absorbed.

2 Mix together the dressing ingredients and leave to stand.

3 Heat a little oil in a frying pan and fry the onions and courgettes until they become soft.

4 Add the chicken and mushrooms. Fry until the chicken is no longer pink.

5 Add the tomatoes, olives and dressing and mix together.

6 Mix together with the couscous.

Ginger Chicken Stir-Fry

NOTE: Omit the chilli, or add less, if you have younger children who don't like spice.

WHERE ON EARTH: Sesame oil is usually found with the other oils. Straight-to-wok noodles can be found in the "world food" section. If you want to use fresh noodles, they are kept in the salad section.

¼ mug **water**

2 tablespoons **white wine vinegar**

6 **spring onions**, sliced

2 tablespoons **honey**

2 tablespoons **soy sauce (GF option)**

1 tablespoon grated, **fresh ginger**

1 fat **red chilli**, deseeded and finely chopped

2 tablespoons **toasted sesame oil**

3 **chicken breasts**, cut into strips

2 medium **yellow or red peppers**, cut into small bite-sized strips

5 **mushrooms**, sliced

400g pack fresh or **straight-to-wok noodles**

1 tablespoon **fresh coriander**, chopped

1 In a medium bowl, stir together the water, vinegar, spring onions, honey, soy sauce, ginger, chilli and cornflour.

2 Heat the sesame oil in a wok and add the chicken. Fry until it is no longer pink. Add the peppers and mushrooms and fry for a minute.

3 Add the onion mixture and heat through. Add the noodles and heat through. Sprinkle over with chopped coriander and serve.

BEN & NICOLE: "Although there were lots of ingredients that would normally have put me off cooking it, it was really worth the extra effort. I really enjoyed cooking it and felt like it made me a better cook. Oh my! Did it taste good!"

Chicken Tetrazzini

NOTE: Poaching is a great way to cook chicken, it is really easy and keeps the chicken lovely and tender. If, when you come to cut it, it is not cooked through, simply put back in the water and bring to the boil again and then it should be fine.

2 **chicken breasts**

1 head of **broccoli**

2½ mugs **pasta shells**

2 **carrots**, thinly sliced

75g **butter** (measure using packet)

2 tablespoons **flour**

600ml or 2 mugs **milk**

¼ mug double **cream**

1 **chicken stock pot/cube**

1 tablespoon chopped **fresh basil**, or 1 teaspoon **dried basil**

1 mug grated **cheese**

½ mug **pine nuts**

1 Grease a large casserole dish.

2 Fill a small pan with boiling water, add the chicken breasts and bring back to the boil. Turn the heat off and put a lid on the pan. Leave for 15 minutes.

3 Cut the very tops off the broccoli and chop the stem into small pieces.

4 Put the pasta on to cook with the stem of the broccoli and the sliced carrots. Cook for 5 minutes. Add the broccoli heads and cook for a further 5 minutes. Drain everything and return to the pan.

5 To make the sauce, melt the butter in a pan and add the flour. Mix together. Add the milk, cream and stock and gently bring to the boil, stirring all the time. The sauce should thicken. Season well and add the basil.

6 Cut the cooked chicken into bite-sized pieces. Mix the chicken, pasta and vegetables with the sauce and pour into the casserole dish.

7 Mix the cheese and pine nuts together and sprinkle over the casserole. Place under a hot grill until the cheese is browned.

Watch a video of making a roux sauce
noshbooks.com/roux

£ 1.16 /PERSON   SERVES 4   EASE ★★☆☆☆   PREP 25 MINS   OK TO FREEZE   GF OPTION

Creamy Tomato Chicken

oil to fry

1 small **onion**, chopped

1 clove **garlic**, finely chopped

2 large **chicken breasts**, cut into thin strips

8 **mushrooms**, sliced

3 **tomatoes**, chopped

½ x 300ml carton **double cream**

½ **chicken stock pot/cube (GF option)**

1 tablespoon **tomato purée**

250g **spaghetti or tagliatelli (GF option)**

2 tablespoons **freshly chopped basil**

1 Put the spaghetti on to cook (see page 17).

2 Fry the onion and garlic until the onion begins to soften.

3 Add the chicken and fry until no longer pink.

4 Add the mushrooms and tomato. Fry for 1–2 minutes.

5 Add the cream, stock, tomato purée and season with salt and pepper. Bring to boil and then turn down to simmer for 2 minutes.

6 Serve with the pasta and basil.

Crispy Fried Lamb

500g **lamb mince**

1 **red onion**, sliced

1 clove **garlic**, chopped

2 medium **carrots**, coarsely grated (in a processor if you have one)

2 medium **courgettes**, chopped

2 tablespoons **balsamic vinegar**

½ mug **water**

1 **lamb** or **vegetable stock pot/cube (GF option)**

1 dessertspoon **honey**

1 tablespoon freshly chopped **mint** or 1 teaspoon **dried mint**

1 Put the baked potatoes in the oven to cook.

2 Heat a large frying pan. Add the lamb mince and cook on a fairly high heat until it is browned and crispy. Stir frequently.

3 Add the onion, garlic, carrots and courgettes and cook until the onions begin to soften.

4 Add the vinegar, water and stock cube. Put a lid over (or foil) and simmer gently for 5 minutes, or until the carrot is tender. Add more water if things get dry.

5 Take off the heat and add the honey and mint. Stir and season well with salt and pepper.

6 Serve with baked potatoes.

One-Pot Chicken Korma

NOTE: If you like things spicy, you can add an extra tablespoon of curry paste, or use a hotter paste like Madras.

ONE MORE THING: Minimal washing up with this one as you only have to use one pot.

1 tablespoon **oil**, to fry

2 **onions**, sliced

2 cloves **garlic**, chopped finely

2 **chicken breasts,** cut into bite-sized pieces

1 tablespoon **Korma curry paste (GF option)**

4 **tomatoes**, chopped

1 mug **basmati rice**

2 mugs **water** + 1 **chicken stock pot/cube (GF option)**

1/2 mug **raisins**

1/2 x 100g pack **pine nuts**

100g pack of **fresh spinach**

crème fraîche or natural yogurt, to serve

1 Heat a little oil in a wok. Add the onions and garlic and fry until soft.

2 Add the chicken pieces and cook until no longer pink.

3 Add the curry paste and tomatoes. Fry for 30 seconds.

4 Add the rice and cook for a further 30 seconds.

5 Add the stock, raisins and water. Bring to the boil.

6 Cover with a lid or foil. Turn down to simmer for 10–15 minutes, until most of the water has been absorbed.

7 Add the pine nuts and the fresh spinach. Stir until the spinach is wilted, this should only take 30 seconds or so.

8 Serve with a little yogurt.

JO: "Was not sure the kids would like this but they ate the lot! I have never given them spinach before, Ollie admitted it was OK. We have never eaten pine nuts before, but we liked the texture they gave."

£ 0.91 /PERSON · SERVES 4 · EASE ★★☆☆☆ · PREP 30 MINS · OK TO FREEZE · GF OPTION

Balsamic Chilli Beef Ragu

NOTE: This is a bit of a spin on the classic "spag bol". It has a few more ingredients and a slightly richer flavour.

ONE MORE THING: If you don't have a food processor, just finely chop the carrots, celery, onion and chilli.

2 medium **carrots**, peeled

3 sticks **celery**

1 **onion**, peeled and cut into ¼'s

1 fat **red chilli**, finely chopped, or ½ teaspoon **paprika**

1 clove **garlic**, finely chopped

1 tablespoon **oil**

500g **minced beef**

3 tablespoons **balsamic vinegar**

400g tin **tomatoes**

1 tablespoon **tomato purée**

1 mug **water**

1 **beef stock pot/cube (GF option)**

1 teaspoon **sugar**

2 mugs **penne pasta (GF option)**

1 tablespoon freshly chopped **basil**

Parmesan cheese (optional)

1 Put the carrots, celery, onion, chilli and garlic in a food processor and blitz.

2 Heat a little oil in a large pan and add the vegetables, cooking for 3–4 minutes.

3 Add the mince to the pan and cook until no longer pink. Add the balsamic vinegar and cook for 1 minute.

4 Add the tomatoes, tomato purée, water, stock and sugar. Bring to the boil and then leave to simmer for 10 minutes.

5 Meanwhile, cook the pasta (see page 17). Once cooked, drain, but retain some of the cooking liquid.

6 Add the pasta to the meat sauce and stir well. If necessary, add some of the pasta water. The sauce should be quite wet. Add the fresh basil and stir in.

7 To serve, grate a little Parmesan over the top.

£2.08 /PERSON | SERVES 4 | EASE ★★★☆☆ | PREP 30 MINS | COOK 25 MINS | OK TO FREEZE ❄

Crunchy Topped Tuna Bake

NOTE: This is a bit of a posh tuna bake. However, it is still inexpensive. The crispy topping is a winner with the kids too.

2 mugs **pasta**, (penne, farfalle, etc.)

2 x 185g tins **tuna**, drained

1/2 x 300g pack **mushrooms**, sliced

1/2 x 250g pack of **cherry tomatoes**, halved

Cheese sauce

50g **butter** (measure on packet)

2 heaped tablespoons **flour**

2 mugs **milk** (1 pint)

1 mug grated **cheese**

salt and **pepper**

Topping

1/2 mug grated **cheese**

2 slices of wholemeal bread, made into **breadcrumbs**

green salad to serve

1 Preheat the oven to 180ºC fan oven/200ºC/gas 6. Lightly grease a large casserole dish.

2 Cook the pasta, drain and leave until needed.

3 To make the cheese sauce, put the butter in a saucepan and gently melt. Add the flour and stir well, cook for 30 seconds. Add the milk and stir well. Bring to the boil, stirring frequently (a small whisk works well for this). Add the cheese. The sauce should thicken. Season well.

4 Put the tuna, mushrooms, tomato and pasta in the bottom of the casserole dish. Gently fold things around a bit, but don't stir, as the tuna will go mushy. Season well with pepper and a little salt to taste.

5 Pour the cheese sauce evenly over the top. Sprinkle over with the grated cheese and breadcrumbs.

6 Place in the oven for 25 minutes until the top is nicely browned.

7 Serve with a green salad.

PETER & BERNICE:
"Nice, tasty and easy recipe. Everyone liked it."

Watch a video of making a roux sauce at
noshbooks.com/roux

something for the weekend

Weekends are times to relax and not rush around so much. Lots of the recipes here need time to cook in the oven, but you will end up with some delicious food. I have also included some breakfast ideas for those relaxed Saturday and Sunday mornings when you don't have work, or have the school-run to contend with. Ideal for getting the kids involved.

£0.59 /PERSON

SERVES 4

EASE ★★☆☆☆

PREP 20 MINS

COOK 40 MINS

Simple Saturday Brunch

NOTE: This is great for chilling out on a Saturday morning when everyone has got up a little late. Cooking the sausages and bacon in the oven avoids you having to stand around too many frying pans in your pyjamas and smelling like a 'greasy spoon cafe' when you go to bed later that day!

4 **sausages**

8 rashers of **bacon**

Eggie bread

4 slices of **bread**

2 **eggs**, beaten

oil or **butter** to fry

400g tin **baked beans**

1 Preheat the oven to 180ºC fan oven/200ºC/gas 6. Grease 2 baking trays.

2 Place the sausages on one tray and place in the oven for 40 minutes.

3 10 minutes into the cooking time, place the bacon on the other tray and place in the oven. Cook for the remaining 30 minutes.

4 About 10 minutes before the end of the cooking time for the sausages, place the beaten eggs on a large plate and season well. Dip both sides of each slice of bread in the egg mixture. Make sure each side is completely covered in egg.

5 Heat a little oil, or butter, in a frying pan. Add the bread and cook for 1–2 minutes, each side, until the egg is browned.

6 Serve with the sausages, bacon and cooked beans.

£0.63 /PERSON — SERVES 4 — EASE ★★☆☆☆ — PREP 30 MINS

American Breakfast Pancakes

NOTE: Poaching eggs is easy if you have gently simmering water in the frying pan. See video link below.

Pancakes

1½ mugs **self-raising flour**

¼ mug **sugar**

4 **eggs**

½ mug **milk**

white Flora to fry

8 rashers of **bacon**

4 **eggs**

maple syrup to serve

1   Put the flour, sugar, eggs and milk in a bowl and mix well, or put everything in a food processor. It should be thicker than a normal pancake mix.

2   Heat a little white Flora in a frying pan. Once hot, add the pancake mix, 3 tablespoons at a time, in order to make small pancakes. No need to spread out the mixture. Cook one at a time. This mixture should make around 6 pancakes.

3   Keep the pancakes warm on a plate with some foil over the top. Fry or grill the bacon until crispy.

4   Poach the eggs at the same time. Put some boiling water into a large frying pan. Bring to simmering point. Break an egg into a cup, lower into the boiling water and gently pour out. Repeat the process with each egg. You may find it necessary to spoon over the yoke with some of the boiling water to fully cook the egg. Simmer until the white of the egg is fully cooked.

5   Serve with the maple syrup and crispy bacon.

BEN & NICOLE: "We like to do this for special breakfasts every now and then. Don't knock the maple syrup and bacon 'til you try it. One of my best food discoveries of the year."

Watch a video of poaching eggs at
noshbooks.com/poaching-eggs

Egg-Fried Ploughman's

8 slices of **wholemeal bread or white**, buttered

1½ mugs grated **Cheddar**

pickles or sliced tomatoes

4 **eggs**, beaten and seasoned with **salt** and **pepper**

butter to fry

1 Preheat the oven to 160ºC fan oven/180ºC/gas 5.

2 Make up the sandwiches with the cheese and either the sliced tomatoes or the pickle.

3 Pour ½ the beaten eggs onto a large plate and dip 2 of the sandwiches into the egg, allowing the egg to soak up a little on each side. Repeat with the rest of the egg and the other two sandwiches.

4 Heat the butter in the pan and fry the sandwiches on a low heat, on each side, until browned. The cheese will also melt in the middle. Repeat with all the sandwiches, storing them in the preheated oven to keep warm.

5 Serve with a little salad.

£0.53 /PERSON   SERVES 4   EASE ★★★☆☆   PREP 30 MINS   V

Blueberry Pancakes with Caramel Sauce

Caramel Sauce

100g **butter** (measure using packet)

4 tablespoons **brown sugar**

1/2 x 300ml pot **double cream**

3 **eggs**

1/4 mug **sugar**

1¼ mugs **self-raising flour**

1/4 mug **milk**

1/4 x 400g pack of **frozen blueberries or raspberries,** defrosted

white Flora to fry

1 Make the caramel sauce by putting the ingredients in a small saucepan and bringing to the boil. Simmer for 30 seconds and then set to one side until needed.

2 Beat the eggs, sugar and flour together and then add the milk to make a thick creamy consistency.

3 Drain the blueberries and add just before you begin to cook the pancakes.

4 Heat a little white Flora in a frying pan. Add about a tablespoon of the pancake mix and allow it to spread in the pan. You should get three in the pan at one time. Cook on a medium heat. Leave to cook on one side and then flip over to lightly brown the other side. Repeat until all the pancakes are cooked.

5 Serve with the caramel sauce, or maple syrup.

Salmon Cakes with Hoisin Dip

NOTE: You can freeze the salmon cakes before you cook them, then defrost and fry them when you need them.

ONE MORE THING: You could add a chopped red chilli to the sauce if you like your food more spicy.

2 large **potatoes,** peeled and cut into 2cm chunks

400g **salmon fillet**

3 **spring onions,** chopped

1 **egg yolk**

½ x 340g tin **sweetcorn**

2 **eggs,** beaten

2 tablespoons **flour**

3 slices of **wholemeal bread,** made into breadcrumbs

1 tablespoon **oil**

salad to serve

Dipping Sauce

1 dessertspoon **oil**

2 **spring onions,** chopped

2 tablespoons **hoisin sauce**

1 teaspoon **soy sauce**

2 teaspoons **cornflour**

1 teaspoon **sugar**

1 Add the potatoes to boiling water, with a little salt, and simmer for 10 minutes. 5 minutes before the end of the cooking time, add the salmon fillet to the pan.

2 Meanwhile, make the sauce. Heat the oil in a small saucepan, add the 2 spring onions and fry for 1 minute. Mix together the rest of the sauce ingredients in a mug. Add enough water to make one mug of liquid and then add to the pan. Bring to the boil, the sauce should thicken.

3 Once the potatoes and the salmon are cooked, drain. Take out the salmon, remove the skin and flake the fish into a bowl. Mash the potatoes and stir in the fish.

4 Heat a little oil in a frying pan and fry the 3 spring onions for 1–2 minutes until they begin to soften.

5 Add the onions to the potatoes and fish, along with the sweetcorn and egg yolk. Season well with salt and pepper. Mix together.

6 Form the mixture into 8–10 cakes and place on a floured board.

7 Put the beaten egg in a shallow dish. Dip the formed cakes in the egg and then into the breadcrumbs.

8 Heat the oil in a frying pan and, once hot, add the salmon cakes. You may have to fry in 2 batches. Cook on a medium heat for 2–3 minutes each side, or until the cakes are browned and crispy on the outside.

£ 1.51 /PERSON   SERVES 4   EASE ★★★☆☆   PREP 30 MINS   COOK 50 MINS   GF OPTION

Barbeque Chicken with Apple Salad

NOTE: The salad with this one is a little different. Do give it a try, but if you don't like the combination of potato wedges and salad, it is also great with corn on the cob.

Why not try out some other salads from page 28.

8 **chicken thighs**

4 medium **potatoes**, cut into wedges

oil

BBQ sauce

1 clove **garlic**

3 **sun-dried tomatoes**, chopped + 1 tablespoon of the oil from the jar

3 tablespoons **soy sauce**

2 tablespoons **honey**

1 tablespoon **tomato purée**

salt and **pepper**

Salad

1 **little gem lettuce**

2 sticks **celery**

8cm piece of **cucumber**

2 **spring onions**

½ **fennel** bulb

1 **red apple**, cored

Dressing

juice of a ½ **lemon** or 1 tablespoon **balsamic vinegar**

1 tablespoon **olive oil**

1 teaspoon **sugar**

1 tablespoon freshly chopped **basil** or 1 teaspoon **dried basil**

salt and **pepper**

1   Preheat the oven to 180ºC fan oven/200ºC/gas 6.

2   Put the chicken thighs in a large, greased casserole dish. Put in the oven for 25 minutes.

3   Mix the BBQ sauce ingredients together in a food processor. After the chicken thighs have been cooked for 25 minutes, take them out of the oven and spread the sauce over them. Return to the oven for a further 25 minutes until browned.

4   Meanwhile, put the potato wedges on a roasting tray and sprinkle with oil and salt and pepper. Distribute well. Put in the oven for 35–40 minutes.

5   Slice the salad ingredients in the food processor, or thinly slice by hand. Add the dressing just before serving.

Moroccan Lamb Pie

NOTE: If you have a hob-to-oven casserole dish, this is a one-pot meal.

4 large **potatoes** (no need to peel) cut into 2cm cubes

25g **butter** (measure using packet)

1 tablespoon **oil**

1 **onion**, sliced

2 medium **carrots**, cut into small pieces

1 teaspoon freshly grated **ginger**

1 clove **garlic**, finely chopped

500g pack **lamb mince**

1 teaspoon ground **cumin**

1 teaspoon ground **coriander**

¹/₂ teaspoon **paprika**

400g tin **chopped tomatoes**

1 **lamb** or **vegetable stock pot/ cube (GF option)**

1 mug **water**

1 Preheat the oven to 180ºC fan oven/200ºC/gas 6.

2 Put the potatoes in boiling water and simmer for 10 minutes. Drain and return to pan. Add the butter and stir. Crush with a potato masher, but do not completely mash.

3 Heat the oil in a hob-to-oven casserole or large saucepan and add the onion, carrots, ginger and garlic. Fry until the onions begin to soften.

4 Add the mince and fry until it is no longer pink.

5 Add the cumin, coriander and paprika. Cook for 30 seconds.

6 Add the tomatoes, stock and water and bring to the boil. Once boiling, season well. Pour into a casserole dish if you have not used a hob-to-oven casserole.

7 Spread the crushed potatoes over the top of the mince mixture and place in the oven, without a lid, for 30 minutes, until the potatoes are browned a little.

STEVE & CANDY: "Really enjoyed cooking with lamb mince and doing something with it that I have not previously cooked. Great family meal."

100

£ 1.47 /PERSON | SERVES 6 | EASE ★★☆☆☆ | PREP 30 MINS | COOK 90 MINS | OK TO FREEZE | GF OPTION

Sweet Pork and Apple Stew

NOTE: Good one-pot dish, which includes all the vegetables you will need for a full meal.

2 tablespoons olive **oil**

2 **onions**, sliced

1 **leek**, sliced

4 **carrots**, sliced

2 cloves **garlic**, finely chopped

1kg **diced pork shoulder**

1 tablespoon **flour (GF option)**

2 **Cox's apples**, cored and cut into chunks

1 mug **apple juice**

2 tablespoons **cider vinegar**

1 mug **water**

2 **vegetable stock pot/ cubes (GF option)**

3 sprigs **fresh thyme**, or 1 teaspoon **dried thyme**

4 large **potatoes** (no need to peel), cut into 2cm cubes

1 Preheat the oven to 180ºC fan oven/200ºC/gas 6.

2 Heat the oil in a hob-to-oven casserole. Add the onions, leeks, carrots and garlic. Fry until they begin to brown.

3 Add the pork and fry until it is no longer pink on the outside.

4 Add the flour and mix well. Add the apples, apple juice, cider vinegar, water, stock and thyme and bring to the boil. The sauce should thicken a little. Season well. Add the fresh thyme.

5 Take off the heat and arrange the cubed potatoes on the top. Season well with salt and pepper.

6 Place in the oven, with the lid on, for 60 minutes. Take the lid off and cook for a further 30–35 minutes until the potatoes are browned.

£ 1.47 /PERSON · SERVES 4 · EASE ★★★☆☆ · PREP 30 MINS · COOK 25 MINS · OK TO FREEZE · GF OPTION

Beef and Bacon Bake

NOTE: Great one-pot dish if you have a hob-to-oven casserole dish.

1 tablespoon **oil**

8 slices of **streaky bacon,** chopped

1 **red pepper**, chopped

1 **onion**, sliced

2 cloves **garlic**, finely chopped

500g **beef mince**

1 mug **basmati rice**

1½ mugs **water**

6 **tomatoes**, chopped

1 tablespoon **tomato purée**

1 **beef stock pot/cube (GF option)**

1 tablespoon freshly chopped **basil,** or 1 teaspoon **dried basil**

1 mug grated **cheese**

1 Preheat the oven to 180ºC fan oven/200ºC/ gas 6.

2 Heat the oil in a hob-to-oven casserole and add the bacon, peppers, onions and garlic. Fry until they begin to brown.

3 Add the mince and cook until it is no longer pink.

4 Add the rice and cook for 30 seconds.

5 Add the water, tomatoes, tomato purée, stock and basil. Season well. Bring to the boil.

6 Take off the heat and sprinkle the grated cheese over the top. Place in the oven for 20–25 minutes until the cheese is browned.

ANDY & HEATHER: "I really like one-pot dishes, especially when it comes to clearing up. This is an original idea, cooking rice in the dish. It's really tasty."

Scrumpy Pork Pie

NOTE: No need to cut the edges off the pastry. Just loosely lay it over the top and scrunch it in a little. This way you don't have to faff about with crimping and there is much more pastry to go around.

---

4 large **potatoes**, cut into 2cm cubes

1 tablespoon **oil**

oil to fry

1 **onion**, sliced

1 clove **garlic**, finely chopped

2 sticks **celery**, sliced

1 large **sweet potato**, cut into 2cm cubes

500g **pork mince**

2 tablespoons **flour**

1 mug (½ pint) **cider**

1 **vegetable stock pot/cube**

1 teaspoon dried **thyme**, or 3-4 **fresh sprigs**

½ mug **water**

1 sheet **ready-rolled puff pastry**

1 beaten **egg**

green veg to serve

1 Preheat the oven to 200ºC fan oven/220ºC/gas 7. Grease a large casserole dish.

2 Put the cubed potatoes on a baking tray and sprinkle the tablespoon of oil over. Season with salt and pepper and distribute the oil evenly with your hands.

3 Heat a little oil in a large pan or wok. Add the onions and garlic and fry for 1 minute. Add the celery and sweet potatoes and fry for 1 minute.

4 Add the pork mince and fry until the meat is no longer pink.

5 Add the flour and cook for 1 minute, stirring frequently.

6 Add the cider, stock, thyme and water. Season well with salt and pepper. Bring to the boil and the sauce should thicken. Turn down to simmer, for 10 minutes, with a lid on the pan.

7 Put the potatoes in the oven for 30–35 minutes.

8 Pour the pork mixture into the casserole dish. Unroll the pastry and place over the top of the pork. Brush the top with beaten egg and pierce a hole in the centre to let out the steam.

9 Place in the oven for 25 minutes, until the pastry is cooked and browned on top. Serve with the potatoes and green veg.

BEN & NICOLE: "I thought pie with pastry was supposed to be difficult. Great idea to use ready-made puff pastry, really tasty too. We all cleared our plates."

Honey Sesame Chicken with Carrot Salad

NOTE: These chicken thighs could also go really well with the "Sweet Potato Rice" from page 116, or the "Potato salad" from page 28.

WHERE ON EARTH: Sesame seeds are kept near the baking section of the supermarket.

4 medium **potatoes** cut into 2cm chunks

oil

oil to fry

8 medium-sized **chicken thighs**

2 tablespoons **honey**

1 tablespoon **sesame seeds**

BBQ Sauce

1 **onion**, chopped

1 clove **garlic,** chopped finely

400g tin **chopped tomatoes**

1 tablespoon **Worcestershire sauce**

1 tablespoon **tomato purée**

1 teaspoon **paprika**

1 teaspoon **sugar**

Carrot and Apple Salad

3 medium **carrots**, grated

3 **red apples**, cored and grated

1/2 bunch of **spring onions,** chopped

handful of fresh **basil leaves**, chopped

juice of 1/2 **lemon**

1 tablespoon **olive oil**

1 Preheat the oven to 200ºC fan oven/220ºC/gas 7.

2 Put the potatoes on a large baking tray, drizzle with oil and season with salt and pepper. Distribute the oil around with your hands. Put in the oven for 25–30 minutes.

3 Put a little oil in a large frying pan and fry the chicken thighs on a medium heat, skin side down, for about 10 minutes. Turn them over and cover with a lid and cook on the flesh side for about 6 minutes.

4 Meanwhile, make the BBQ sauce. Heat a little oil in a saucepan and fry the onions and garlic until the onions begin to soften. Add the rest of the ingredients and bring to the boil. Simmer gently for 5 minutes.

5 Make the carrot salad by simply mixing the ingredients together and season well. Set aside.

6 Turn the chicken thighs over and sprinkle with the honey and sesame seeds. Turn over and fry on the skin side for 2–3 minutes until the honey is really browned. Be careful not to burn them at this stage.

7 Everything should be ready to serve together.

Beef and Tomato Pie with Potato Crush

NOTE: For shortcrust pastry, the oven should be at 180ºC fan oven/200ºC/gas 6.

1 tablespoon **oil** to fry

1 **onion**, sliced

500g **minced beef**

6 large **tomatoes,** each cut into 8

1 tablespoon **flour**

1 mug **water**

1 clove **garlic**, finely chopped

1 teaspoon **sugar**

1 sprig of fresh **rosemary**

1 **beef stock pot/cube**

1 pack **puff pastry** or make your own short-crust (see page 32)

1 beaten **egg**

Potato crush

4 large **potatoes** (no need to peel), cut into 4cm chunks

25g **butter** (measure using packet)

1 mug grated **cheddar cheese**

green beans to serve

1 Preheat the oven to 200ºC fan oven/220ºC/gas 7.

2 Heat a little oil in a large pan, or wok, and fry the onions until they begin to brown.

3 Add the minced beef and fry until quite browned. This will take about 5 minutes, but will add lots of flavour.

4 Add the tomatoes to the pan and cook for 1 minute.

5 Add the flour and stir well. Add the water, garlic, sugar, rosemary and stock and bring to the boil. Season well and place in a casserole dish.

6 Unroll the pastry and place over the meat (see photo). Brush the top with beaten egg.

7 Place in the oven for 20–25 minutes until the pastry is nicely browned.

8 Meanwhile, put the potatoes in a pan of boiling water, bring to the boil and then turn down to simmer for 10 minutes. Once they are cooked, drain and return to the pan.

9 Cook the beans.

10 Crush, once around in the pan, with a potato masher. Add the butter, season well and stir. Then add the cheese, but only stir around once, so the cheese is not too mixed in. Serve with the pie.

Creamy Pork and Mushroom Stew

NOTE: Not peeling potatoes saves time and energy. There are many nutrients in the skin of the potato, so you can comfort yourself that, by leaving the skin intact, you are giving your family some extra goodness.

1 tablespoon **oil**

4 slices of **unsmoked, streaky bacon**, chopped

1 **onion**, sliced

750g **pork shoulder,** cut into cubes, or stewing pork

1 tablespoon **flour (GF option)**

1½ mugs **water**

1 mug/300ml **double cream**

8 **mushrooms**, sliced

1 clove **garlic**, chopped

1 **vegetable stock pot/cube (GF option)**

1 tablespoon freshly chopped **parsley** or 1 teaspoon **dried parsley**

2 sprigs of **fresh thyme** or ½ teaspoon **dried thyme**

5 medium **potatoes**, (no need to peel) cut into 3cm chunks

50g **butter** (measure using packet)

6 **carrots,** sliced

1 head broccoli

1 Preheat the oven to 180ºC fan oven/200ºC/gas 6.

2 Heat the oil in a hob-to-oven casserole and fry the bacon and the onions until they begin to brown.

3 Add the cubed meat and cook until it is no longer pink on the outsides. Add the flour and mix well.

4 Add the water, cream, mushrooms, garlic, stock, parsley and thyme. Bring to the boil and then take off the heat. Season well with salt and pepper.

5 Place in the oven, with a lid on, for 1½ hours.

6 When the casserole is almost done, put the potatoes in boiling water, bring to the boil and then turn down to simmer for 10 minutes. Put the carrots and broccoli on to cook at the same time.

7 Drain the potatoes and return to the pan. Crush them with a potato masher, so that lots of them stay almost whole. Add the butter, allow to melt and then give just one stir.

Chicken Chapatis

NOTE: Add a little more chilli powder, if you like your food spicy.

WHERE ON EARTH: Chapatis are usually in the 'bread section' next to tortilla wraps and pitta bread.

Marinade

1 clove **garlic**, finely chopped

1 teaspoon **cumin**

1 teaspoon **turmeric**

1 teaspoon **coriander**

½ teaspoon **chilli powder**

1 tablespoon of freshly grated **ginger**

2 tablespoons **oil**

3 **chicken breasts** cut into strips

6 **chapatis**

1 small **little gem lettuce**, cut into strips

2 **spring onions**, chopped

Raita

300ml tub of **Greek yogurt**

1 tablespoon freshly chopped **mint**

¼ **cucumber**, chopped into small cubes

Tomato chutney (you could use ready-made mango chutney)

1 tablespoon **oil**

1 **onion**, sliced

1 eating **apple**, unpeeled and chopped into small cubes

2 **tomatoes**, chopped

1 tablespoon **white wine vinegar**

1 tablespoon **sugar**

1 Mix the garlic, cumin, tumeric, coriander, chilli powder, ginger and oil in a bowl. Add the chicken pieces and mix. Leave to stand.

2 Meanwhile, make the chutney. Heat the oil in a small saucepan, add the onions and fry until they begin to brown. Add the apples and tomatoes and cook gently for 4–5 minutes. Add the vinegar and sugar and cook for a further 2 minutes. Set to one side until needed.

3 Mix together the raita ingredients.

4 Heat a little oil in a large frying pan and add the chicken pieces. Cook for 2–3 minutes.

5 Serve on the chapatis with the salad, raita and chutney.

STEVE & CANDY:
"Loved these. I used the leftover chutney on a cheese sandwich."

£ 1.73 /PERSON · SERVES 4 · EASE ★★★★★ · PREP 45 MINS · OK TO FREEZE ❄ · GF OPTION

Lamb Meatballs with Sweet Potato Rice

NOTE: If you want this to go a bit further, add 1 slice of wholemeal bread, made into breadcrumbs, to the meatball mix.

ONE MORE THING: You can prepare the meatballs and tomato sauce beforehand (during baby's nap time) and store in the fridge.

Meatballs

500g **lamb mince**

1 tablespoon **curry paste** (mild or hot, depending on taste) (GF option)

1 **egg yolk**

1/2 grated **onion**

oil to fry

Tomato sauce

oil to fry

1 **onion**, sliced

1/2 **fresh red chilli**, deseeded and chopped finely (optional)

1 clove **garlic**, chopped

6 **tomatoes**, chopped or a 400g tin **chopped tomatoes**

1 dessertspoon **tomato purée**

1 teaspoon **sugar**

salt and **pepper**

Sweet Potato Rice

1 large **sweet potato**, peeled and cut into 1cm cubes

1 tablespoon **oil**

1½ mugs **basmati rice**

3 mugs boiling **water**

1 teaspoon **pilau rice seasoning**

1 Preheat the oven to 200ºC fan oven/220ºC/gas 7.

2 Put the sweet potatoes on a baking tray and sprinkle with the oil and season well. Mix with your hands to distribute the oil and seasoning. Place in the oven for 25–30 minutes until browned.

3 To make the sauce, heat the oil in a saucepan and fry the onions until they begin to soften. Add the rest of the ingredients and bring to the boil. Simmer for 5 minutes. Blitz with a hand-held blender. Set aside until needed.

4 Mix together the meatball ingredients (hands work the best). Form into approximately 20 balls.

5 Put the rice on to cook (see page 16).

6 Heat a little oil in a frying pan and fry the meatballs. Leave to brown and then turn, until all sides are browned. Should take 8–10 minutes.

7 Once the rice is cooked, mix in the roasted sweet potatoes.

8 Serve the rice with the meatballs and the tomato sauce.

old classics

We all want the comfort of cooking the familiar and well-loved old classics: Stew and Dumplings, Shepherds Pie, Toad in the Hole, etc.. Maybe they remind us of the days when mum cooked them for us and we did not have to do all the work! There are also step-by-step timings for Roast Chicken dinner which will, hopefully, be of help.

£0.92 /PERSON · SERVES 4 · EASE ★★★★★ · PREP 30 MINS · COOK 3½ HRS · OK TO FREEZE · GF

Slow-Cook Roast Pork

NOTE: When choosing pork for this recipe, don't avoid the pieces of meat with fat in them. The fat contains lots of flavour and you can skim off the excess from the surface of the liquid before making the gravy.

ONE MORE THING: If you want to make crackling, take the skin off the pork and place it on a greased baking tray. Put in the oven with the potatoes and it will be good and crisp after 25 minutes.

1kg piece of **pork shoulder**

1 eating **apple**, cored and cut into 8

1 **onion**, cut into 8

1 teaspoon **fennel seeds**

2 mugs **water**

4 large **potatoes**, peeled and cut into 4cm chunks

6 **carrots**, peeled and cut into 4cm pieces

2 tablespoons **oil**

1 head of **broccoli**

25g softened **butter** (measure using packet)

1 tablespoon **flour**

1 Preheat the oven to 180ºC fan oven/200ºC/gas 6.

2 Put the pork, apple, onion, water and fennel seeds into a large casserole dish. Season with salt and pepper. Place the lid on the casserole and put in the oven for 30 minutes. After 30 minutes, turn the heat down to 150ºC fan oven/170ºC/gas 3 and cook for a further 3¹/2 hours.

3 30 minutes before the end of the cooking time, put the potatoes and carrots in a pan of boiling water. Bring to the boil and simmer for 10 minu256tes. While they are cooking, put a roasting tin in the oven, with the oil in, to heat up. Drain the potatoes, but retain the cooking water for the gravy.

4 Take the meat out of the oven and turn the oven up to 200ºC fan oven/220ºC/gas 7.

5 Take the roasting tray out and tip the potatoes and carrots into the tray. Carefully turn over the veg to coat with the oil. Return to the oven for 25–30 minutes, until the veg is browned.

6 Pour the liquid out of the casserole dish into a saucepan. Leave the meat in the casserole to keep warm. In a bowl, mix the butter and the flour together to make a paste. Add to the saucepan and stir well. Bring to the boil; the gravy should thicken. Add some of the potato water if necessary. Taste and, if needed, add some vegetable stock (cube or concentrated liquid). Set to one side until needed.

7 Put the broccoli in a pan of boiling water and simmer for 5 minutes.

PETER & BERNICE: "This is now a family favourite - very popular. Good to have something you can safely leave in the oven and go out for a while, come back and it's cooked."

One-Pot Beef Cobbler

NOTE: This is a really homely dish. Great for winter evenings to warm your cockles!

WHERE ON EARTH: Suet can be found with the flour in the 'baking section' of the supermarket.

1 tablespoon **oil**

2 **onions**, sliced

500g **beef mince**

4 medium **carrots**, chopped small

1 tablespoon **flour**

1 mug defrosted **frozen peas**

6 **mushrooms**, sliced

2 mugs **water** + 1 **beef stock pot/cube**

1 teaspoon dried **mixed herbs**

salt and **pepper**

Dumpling Topping

1½ mugs **self-raising flour**

¾ mug **suet**

pinch **salt**

1 teaspoon freeze dried **basil** or **coriander**

¾ mug **water**

1 beaten **egg**

1   Preheat the oven to 180ºC fan oven/200ºC/gas 6.

2   Heat the oil in a hob-to-oven casserole. Fry the onion in the oil until soft.

3   Add the mince and carrots and cook until the meat is no longer pink. Add the flour and stir well.

4   Add the peas, mushrooms, water, stock, herbs, salt and pepper. Stir well and simmer for 10 minutes.

5   To make the dumpling top, put the flour, suet, salt and herbs in a dish and stir well. Add water a little at a time and mix. Add just enough water to make a soft ball.

6   Put some flour onto a board or plate. Turn out the mixture and form a ball.

7   Cut into eight pieces and form each into a ball.

8   Gently place them on the top of the meat mixture and brush the top with beaten egg, or milk, to help it brown.

9   Bake in the oven for 25–30 minutes, or until the crust is browned.

JOE & SARAH: "This was my first time making dumplings. They were suprisingly easy and so very tasty that you would have thought I had spent a lot of time making this dish."

£ 1.84 /PERSON · SERVES 4-6 · EASE ★★★☆☆ · PREP 20 MINS · COOK 90 MINS · OK TO FREEZE · GF OPTION

Beef and Mushroom Casserole

oil to fry

1 **onion**, sliced

1 clove **garlic**, chopped finely

4 rashers of **streaky bacon**, cut into chunks

750g **braising steak**, cut into bite-sized pieces

1 tablespoon **flour (GF option)**

½ x 250g pack **mushrooms**, sliced

2 mugs water

2 **beef stock pots/cube**

1 tablespoon **tomato purée**

2 sprigs fresh **rosemary**

4 large **potatoes**

1 Preheat the oven to 160ºC fan oven/180ºC/gas 4.

2 Heat a little oil in a large pan, or hob-to-oven casserole. Add the onions, garlic and bacon and fry until the onions begin to soften.

3 Add the beef and cook until no longer pink on the outside. Add the flour and stir well.

4 Add the mushrooms, beef stock, tomato purée and rosemary. Season well with salt and pepper. If you have used a saucepan, tip the contents into a casserole dish.

5 Put a lid on the casserole and place in the oven for 1½ hours. Check half way through and stir. Add a little more water if necessary.

6 Put the potatoes in the oven to cook for the last hour of the cooking time.

£1.58 /PERSON · SERVES 6 · EASE ★★☆☆☆ · PREP 30 MINS · COOK 90 MINS · OK TO FREEZE ❄

Simple Beef Curry

oil to fry

2 large **onions**, sliced

1kg **stewing beef**, cubed

2 tablespoons **rogan josh curry paste** (use Madras if you like it hot)

1 **beef stock pot/cube** + 1 mug **boiling water**

400g tin **chopped tomatoes**

rice (see page 16)

yogurt and **naan breads**

1. Preheat the oven to 180ºC fan oven/200ºC/ gas 6.

2. Heat the oil in a large hob-to-oven casserole dish. Fry the onions until they begin to soften.

3. Add the beef and cook until it is no longer pink on the outside. Add the curry paste and cook for 30 seconds.

4. Add the water, stock and tomatoes. Bring to the boil. Put a lid on the pan and place in the oven for 1½ hours.

5. Serve with rice, yogurt and naan bread.

£1.02 /PERSON · SERVES 4 · EASE ★★★★☆ · PREP 15 MINS · COOK 40 MINS · V

Toad in the Hole with Cox's Apples

NOTE: The secret of good "Toad In the Hole" is a hot oven and hot fat!

ONE MORE THING: You could serve with some green vegetables instead of the baked beans. Alternatively, if you want to make gravy from scratch, go to the video link below.

Batter

1 mug **self-raising flour**

4 large **eggs**

pinch of **salt**

1/4 mug **milk** + 1/2 mug **water**

2 tablespoons **white Flora** or **oil**

12 thick **pork sausages**, each cut in half

3 Cox's **apples**, cut into wedges

400g tin **baked beans**

1. Preheat the oven to 230ºC fan oven/250ºC/ gas 9.

2. Put the flour in the bowl and add the eggs, salt and a little of the milk. Mix well, beating with a whisk or a large spoon. Add the rest of the milk and water, or you can put all the batter ingredients in a processor and whizz. The mixture should look as thin as single cream.

3. Put the white Flora in a large roasting tin. Place in the hot oven for 10 minutes. Put the sausages and apples in the hot fat. Return to the oven for 10 minutes.

4. Take the roasting tin out of the oven and pour the batter in. It should bubble around the edges as you pour it in.

5. Put back into the oven and cook for 20–25 minutes, or until browned. The mixture should rise around the edges.

6. Serve with the beans.

PETER & BERNICE: "This is the first time I have made a Yorkshire pudding that has risen. Yippee!"

Watch a video on how to make gravy
noshbooks.com/gravy

Stew and Suet Dumplings

NOTE: This uses just one pot and includes all the veg you need for the meal.

ONE MORE THING: The stew is fine to freeze, but not the dumplings.

WHERE ON EARTH: Suet is in the baking section at the supermarket.

---

oil to fry

2 **onions**, sliced

500g **stewing beef**, cut into small pieces

3 mugs **water** + 2 **beef stock pot/ cubes**

3 **carrots**, sliced

2 **potatoes**, cut into 3cm cubes

1 **courgette**, sliced

1 mug frozen **peas**

3 sticks **celery**, sliced

1 teaspoon dried **mixed herbs**

salt and **pepper**

1 tablespoon **flour**

25g softened **butter** (measure using packet)

Dumplings

1/2 mug **suet**

1 mug **self-raising flour**

1/4 mug **water**

1/4 teaspoon **salt**

2 tablespoons **freshly chopped parsley**

1 Heat a little oil in a large saucepan or wok. Add the onions and fry for 1–2 minutes until they begin to soften.

2 Add the meat and cook until it is no longer pink on the outside. Add the flour and mix.

3 Add the rest of the ingredients and bring to the boil. Put a lid on the pan and turn down to simmer for 1 1/2 hours. You may need to stir occasionally and check that the liquid has not boiled away.

4 Make the dumplings by mixing together the flour, salt and suet in a bowl. Add the water a little at a time, just enough to make a soft dough. Make approximately 9 small balls and set to one side until needed.

5 About 15 minutes before the end of the cooking time, add the dumplings. Replace the lid and cook for the rest of the time.

6 Sprinkle over the chopped parsley.

BEN & NICOLE: "I thought this would be really complicated, but it is so simple. The kids loved it, Toby especially likes the dumplings. One in each hand!"

Watch a video of making dumplings at
noshbooks.com/dumplings

Chicken and Leek Pie

Shortcrust Pastry

2 mugs/340g **self-raising flour**

175g **cold butter** (measure using packet) or **white Flora**

1 beaten **egg** + ¼ mug **water**

¼ teaspoon **salt**

Filling

2 tablespoons **oil**

1 **onion**, chopped

2 **leeks**, sliced

3 **chicken breasts**, cut into bite-sized pieces

6 **mushrooms**, sliced

1 dessertspoon **flour**

300ml pot of **double cream**

½ **mug water** + 1 **chicken stock pot/cube**

salt and **pepper**

1 tablespoon freshly chopped **parsley** or **basil**

1 beaten **egg**, to brush the top

4 medium **potatoes** cut into cubes.

green beans

1 Make the pastry, see page 32.

2 Heat the oven to 180ºC fan oven/200ºC/ gas 6.

3 Put the potatoes on a large baking tray, sprinkle with the oil, season with salt and pepper. Mix together and then spread out. Place in the oven for 45 minutes.

4 Heat the oil in a large saucepan or wok. Fry the onions and leeks until they begin to soften.

5 Add the chicken and the mushrooms and cook until the chicken is no longer pink.

6 Add the flour and mix well. Add the cream and stock. Bring to the boil, the sauce should thicken. Take off the heat, season well with salt and pepper and add the herbs. Transfer to a large casserole dish.

7 Roll out the pastry and place on top of the casserole. Make a small hole in the centre to allow the steam to escape. Pinch the edges and brush with the beaten egg.

8 Place in the oven for 25–30 minutes, the pastry should be slightly browned.

9 5 minutes before the end of the cooking time put the beans on to cook.

BEN & NICOLE: "I have never made pie before. I have always wanted to. This was my first time to make pastry too. Not as difficult as I thought, in fact, quite easy. The pie tasted awesome. Bella is a great fan and has requested that we have this every week."

Watch a video of making pastry at
noshbooks.com/pastry

Ben's Desperate Dan Cow Pie

NOTE: Ever read the Dandy, with Desperate Dan? He famously chowed down on Cow Pie. Although this recipe doesn't have the same charicatured "pastry horns" I think it comes pretty close to what Dan would have eaten! This has been Ben's favourite meal for years. He requests it every year for his birthday.

ONE MORE THING: I would never recommend making puff pastry from scratch, as it takes so long, but making shortcrust is very easy. Give it a go.

---

oil to fry

1 **onion**, sliced

750g **stewing beef**

2 mugs **water**

1 **beef stock pot/cube**

5 **carrots**, sliced

6 medium **potatoes**, cut into 1cm slices (no need to peel)

25g softened **butter** (measure using packet)

1 tablespoon **flour**

Shortcrust Pastry

175g **butter** (measure using packet)

2 mugs/340g **self-raising flour**

1 beaten **egg** + ¼ mug **water**

1 Heat a little oil in a large saucepan and fry the onions until they become soft and a little brown.

2 Add the meat and fry until no longer pink on the outside.

3 Add the 2 mugs of water, stock and carrots and bring to the boil. Put a lid on the pan and turn down to simmer for 1½ hours.

4 Add the potatoes to some boiling water and bring to the boil. Turn down to simmer for 8–10 minutes until the potatoes are tender. Drain and return to the pan.

5 Heat the oven to 180ºC fan oven/200ºC/gas 6.

6 Mix the softened butter and flour together, add to the meat and stir well. The gravy should thicken. If most of the liquid has boiled away, add another mug of water.

7 Pour the meat mixture into the bottom of a large casserole dish. Put the cooked potatoes on top.

8 Make the pastry, see page 32. Roll out the pastry and place over the potatoes. Cut to size and pinch the edges of the pastry. Make a little hole in the centre for the steam to get out. This stops the pastry from going soggy. Brush the top with beaten egg.

9 Place in the oven for 25 minutes, or until the pastry is browned on top.

Watch a video of making pastry at
noshbooks.com/pastry

Spaghetti Bolognese

oil to fry

1 **onion**, chopped

2 cloves **garlic**, chopped

500g **beef mince**

400g tin **chopped tomatoes**

2 tablespoons **tomato purée**

6 **mushrooms**, sliced (optional)

1 teaspoon freeze dried **mixed herbs**

1 teaspoon **sugar**

1 **beef stock pot/cube**

1 tablespoon **Worcestershire sauce** (optional)

    salt and **pepper**

      1/2 x 500g pack **spaghetti**

1 Heat a little oil in a large saucepan and fry the onion and garlic for 1 minute.

2 Add the mince and cook until the meat is no longer pink.

3 Add the tomatoes, tomato purée, mushrooms, herbs and sugar. Crumble the stock cube into the pan and stir well. Bring to boil, then simmer gently for 10 minutes. Season well with salt and pepper.

4 Put the spaghetti on to cook (see page 17).

5 Drain the pasta and add a little olive oil to stop it sticking together. Serve on a plate with the Bolognese sauce on the top. You can grate Parmesan or Cheddar cheese over the top if you like.

£ 1.41 /PERSON · SERVES 4 · EASE ★★☆☆☆ · PREP 25 MINS · COOK 25 MINS · OK TO FREEZE ❄

Easy Shepherd's Pie

2 large **sweet potatoes**, cut into 2cm chunks

2 large white **potatoes**, cut into 2cm chunks

25g **butter** (measure using packet)

1 tablespoon **oil**

1 large **onion**, chopped

500g **lamb mince**

1 tablespoon **flour**

1 mug **water**

1 **lamb** or **vegetable stock pot/cube**

2 tablespoons **Worcestershire sauce**

3-4 sprigs of **fresh thyme** or ½ teaspoon **dried thyme**

salt and **pepper**

1 Preheat the oven to 180ºC fan oven/200ºC/gas 6. Grease a casserole dish.

2 Put the potatoes in boiling water, add salt and simmer for 10 minutes. Drain and return to the pan. Add the butter and squash gently with a potato masher, no need to mash. Stir to distribute the butter. Leave to one side until needed.

3 Heat the oil in a large pan or wok. Add the onion and fry until it begins to brown. Add the mince and fry until it is no longer pink.

4 Add the flour and stir well to distribute. Cook for 30 seconds. Add the water, stock cube, Worcestershire sauce, thyme and season well. Bring to the boil and the sauce should thicken.

5 Pour into the bottom of the casserole dish. Put the potatoes on top and spread them out.

6 Place in the oven for 20–25 minutes until brown.

7 Serve with green vegetables.

Bangers and Sweet Potato Mash

2 large **sweet potatoes**, peeled and cut into 2cm chunks

2 large **white potatoes**, not peeled and cut into 2cm chunks

25g **butter** (measure using packet)

salt and **pepper**

a little **oil**

8–10 large pork **sausages**

1 **onion**, chopped

400g tin **baked beans**

2 tablespoons **Worcestershire sauce**

1 dessertspoon **golden syrup**

¼ mug **water**

salt and **pepper**

1   Put the potatoes in boiling water, bring to the boil and turn down to simmer for 10 minutes. Drain and return to the pan. Add the butter and gently squash the potatoes with a masher, but no need to completely mash. Stir in the butter and distribute well. Season with salt and pepper. Leave in the pan with a lid on, until needed.

2   Heat the oil in a large pan or wok. Fry the sausages until they are browned. Add the onions and fry. Stir frequently. Once the onions begin to soften, add the beans, Worcestershire sauce, syrup, water and salt and pepper. Simmer for 2–3 minutes.

3   Serve with the crushed potato.

Healthy Fish and Chips

4 large **potatoes**, cut into wedges

1 tablespoon **oil**

520g pack of frozen **white fish** (defrosted), or 4 **white fish steaks**

3 slices **wholemeal bread**, made into breadcrumbs (GF option)

1 tablespoon **sesame seeds**

grated rind of a **lemon**

30g melted **butter** (measure using packet)

1 **egg**, beaten

salt and **pepper**

2 mugs **frozen peas**

1 Preheat the oven to 180ºC fan oven/200ºC/gas 6.

2 Place the potatoes on a baking tray. Sprinkle with oil, salt and pepper. Mix everything together and stand the wedges on their skins, this helps them not to stick to the tray. Place in the oven for 35 minutes.

3 Meanwhile, mix together the breadcrumbs, melted butter, lemon zest, sesame seeds, salt and pepper.

4 Put the beaten eggs onto a plate and coat each piece of fish with the egg. Dip them into the breadcrumb mix. Place on another baking tray and place in the oven for 20 minutes. The breadcrumbs should be nicely browned. If you are using thicker fish steaks, you will need to leave them in the oven for 25 minutes.

Lasagna with Added Smoky Bacon

4 rashers of **smoked bacon**, chopped

1 onion, **chopped**

1 carrot, finely **chopped**

2 cloves garlic, **chopped**

500g **minced beef**

400g tin chopped **tomatoes**

1 **beef stock pot/cube**

¼ teaspoon **paprika**

1 tablespoon **tomato purée**

White sauce

50g **butter** (measure using packet)

2 heaped tablespoons **flour**

2 mugs **milk**

2 **mozzarella** balls, torn up

9-12 **lasagna** sheets

1 If you have a food processor, put the bacon, onion, carrot and garlic in the processor and blitz for 30 seconds. There is no need to chop.

2 Heat a little oil in a wok, or large saucepan, and fry the onion, bacon, carrot and garlic until they begin to brown.

3 Add the mince and cook until the meat is no longer pink.

4 Add the tomatoes, tomato purée, stock and paprika. Season well and simmer gently for 10 minutes.

5 Preheat the oven to 180ºC fan oven/200ºC/ gas 6.

6 To make the white sauce, put the butter and flour in a saucepan and gently heat until it forms a paste. Take off the heat and add the milk. Stir with a whisk and return to the heat. Gently bring to the boil, stirring all the time. The sauce will thicken. Season well with salt and pepper.

7 Put half the meat mix in the bottom of a casserole dish and place a layer of lasagna sheets over the top. Pour half the sauce on top, then place another layer of lasagna sheets. Repeat the process again. Place the torn mozzarella on the top and season well.

8 Place in the oven for 20–25 minutes until the cheese is browned.

ANDY & HEATHER:
"Lasagna with a bit of a twist, the children really like the bacon in it."

£1.71 /PERSON · SERVES 6 · EASE ★★★★☆ · PREP 45 MINS · COOK 120 MINS · OK TO FREEZE

Roast Chicken Dinner

3kg **chicken**

1 mug boiling **water**

1 tablespoon **oil**

1 teaspoon **dried rosemary** or a sprig of **fresh rosemary**

6 large **potatoes**, cut into 4cm pieces

6–8 **carrots**

1 piece of **broccoli**

Stuffing

1 **onion**, cut into wedges

1 mug boiling **water**

3 slices of **wholemeal bread**, made into breadcrumbs

1 teaspoon **mixed herbs**

400g **sausage meat** or **skinned sausages**

8 **mushrooms**, sliced

salt and **pepper**

Gravy

25g **butter**, softened (measure using packet)

1 tablespoon **flour**

1 Preheat the oven to 180ºC fan oven/200ºC/ gas 6.

2 Put the chicken in a roasting dish and add the water. Brush the top with oil and sprinkle over with some rosemary. Season with salt and pepper. Put in the oven with lid or foil. Cook for 1 hour. Take off the lid and cook for a further hour.

3 To make the stuffing, put the water and onions in a pan and simmer for 5 minutes. Add the rest of the stuffing ingredients to the pan and mix together. Place in a greased casserole dish. Put in the oven for 75 minutes, or until browned. Stir once during the cooking time.

4 Put the potatoes on a tray and sprinkle with oil and season. Mix together to make sure all the surfaces of the potatoes are covered. Place in the oven for 1 hour.

5 Put the vegetables on to cook. Once cooked, drain, but retain the cooking liquid. Return the vegetables to the pans to keep warm.

6 Take the chicken out after 2 hours and transfer onto a large plate. Cover with foil to keep it warm.

7 In a bowl, mix together the butter and flour to make a paste. Mix some of the carrot water and the juices from the bottom of the roasting tin in a saucepan. Bring to the boil and add the butter and flour mixture. Whisk together and the gravy should thicken.

Timeline

10:45am	11:30am	12:15pm	12:30pm	1:10pm	1:15pm	1:15pm
Chicken in oven	stuffing in oven	stir stuffing, return to oven	potatoes in oven	carrots on (drain once cooked and return to the pan)	chicken out and make gravy	broccoli on to cook

Steak and Ale Casserole

NOTE: If you want to slow cook this while you go out, you can put in the oven for 40 minutes on 180ºC fan oven/200ºC/gas 6, then turn the oven down to 100ºC fan oven/120ºC/gas 1 and cook for a further 3–4 hours.

2 tablespoons **oil**

2 **onions**, sliced

1kg **stewing steak**

3 tablespoons **flour**

400ml bottle of **fruity ale**

2 mugs **water**

2 **beef stock pot/cubes**

3 **celery** sticks, roughly chopped

4 large **carrots**, cut into large chunks

2 large **parsnips**, cut into wedges

4 sprigs of **thyme**

Potato Squash

7 large **potatoes**, (no need to peel) cut into 3cm pieces

50g **butter** (measure using packet)

1 large head of **broccoli**, cut into florets

1/2 x 500g packet of **frozen peas**

salt and **pepper**

1 Preheat the oven to 180ºC fan oven/200ºC/gas 6.

2 Heat the oil in a large hob-to-oven casserole dish. Fry the onions until they begin to soften.

3 Add the meat and cook until the meat is no longer pink on the outside. Stir frequently.

4 Add the flour and stir until it is evenly distributed. Add the ale and stir well.

5 Add the water, ale, stock, celery, carrots, parsnips and thyme. Bring to the boil. Season well

6 Place in the preheated oven for 1½ hours.

7 When the casserole has 30 minutes left to cook, put the potatoes on to boil for 10 minutes. Drain and return to the pan. Add the butter and squash with a potato masher, but don't mash them too much.

8 Put the broccoli and peas on to cook together in the same pan. Once cooked, drain and gently mix into the potato squash.

special days

Having friends around, or you have at last found time to make a special meal to share together? This is the time to 'push the boat out' and find something a bit different. Some may take a bit more effort, others are still very simple to make. All are scrumptious.

Poached Salmon with Mustard Sauce and Cucumber Pickle

NOTE: Lovely meal when you get the chance to eat together, without the kids.

Mustard Sauce

3 tablespoons **crème fraîche**

1 teaspoon **dijon mustard** or wholegrain mustard

1 tablespoon fresh **basil**, chopped

Cucumber Pickle

2 tablespoons **white wine vinegar or white balsamic**

2 tablespoons **olive oil**

1 teaspoon **sugar**

salt and **pepper**

3 spring **onions**, chopped

10cm piece of **cucumber**

2 **salmon fillets**

200g pack **green beans**

1/2 x 1Kg pack **new potatoes**

1 Mix the cream sauce ingredients together in a bowl and set aside until needed.

2 Mix together the wine vinegar, olive oil, sugar and salt and pepper in another bowl. Add the spring onions. Cut the cucumber in half lengthways and scoop out the seed part. Cut into small chunks and add to the bowl.

3 Put a pan of water on to boil. Once boiling, add the potatoes to one and cook for 5 minutes. Add the beans and cook for a further 5 minutes.

4 When they are 5 minutes off cooked, place 1/2 mug of water in a saucepan and bring to the boil. Turn down to simmer. Add the salmon fillets, season with salt and pepper, cover with a lid and simmer for 5 minutes. Gently open up the fish with a fork to check that they are cooked in the middle.

5 Drain the veggies and serve together, as photo.

ALAN & JO: "This is brill, loved the cucumber pickle which was a real surprise. Have made it loads of times."

Thai Coconut Chicken

NOTE: Really quick one-pot dish. Just put everything in together, no need to cook anything on the hob, just straight in the oven.

ONE MORE THING: This makes quite a thin sauce, but is delicious

WHERE ON EARTH: Red Thai curry paste is usually in the speciality foods section at the supermarket.

3 **sweet potatoes**, peeled and cut into 2cm chunks

1 **onion**, cut into wedges

8 **chicken thighs**

1 tin **coconut milk**

1 clove **garlic**, chopped

1 tablespoon grated **ginger**

juice of a **lime**

1 **chicken stock pot/cube (GF option)**

1 tablespoon **red Thai curry paste (GF option)** (more if your kids are older)

rice and **green veg** to serve

1 Preheat the oven to 180ºC fan oven/200ºC/gas 6.

2 Put the sweet potatoes and onions on the bottom of a large casserole dish. Place the chicken thighs on the top.

3 Mix the coconut milk, garlic, ginger, lime juice, stock and curry paste together. Pour over the top of the thighs.

4 Place in the oven, uncovered, for 1 hour. If the chicken thighs begin to brown too much, cover with a piece of foil.

5 Serve with rice (see page 16) and green veg.

JOE & SARAH: "I love cooking Thai and the Crispy Thai chicken was certainly different from the way I would have normally cooked it, but equally, if not, better tasting. I'll certainly be using this recipe again soon."

Watch a video of how to cook rice at
noshbooks.com/rice

Lemon Ginger Chicken

3 **chicken breasts**

juice and grated zest of a **lemon**

1 tablespoon **honey**

1 tablespoon **olive oil**

2 cloves **garlic**, finely chopped

1 tablespoon fresh **ginger**, grated

1½ mugs **rice**

3 mugs **water**

2 teaspoons **pilau rice seasoning**

200g pack mangetout, cut into thin strips

1 Preheat the oven to 180ºC fan oven 200ºC/gas 6. Lightly grease an ovenproof dish.

2 Mix together the lemon zest, juice, honey, garlic, ginger and oil. Place the chicken in the dish and pour the sauce over. Place in the oven for 25 minutes.

3 Meanwhile, put the water in a saucepan and bring to the boil. Add the pilau rice seasoning and the rice. Stir and bring back to the boil. Turn down to simmer, with the lid on, for about 10 minutes, or until the rice is tender and all the liquid absorbed.

4 Once the rice is cooked, add the mangetout to the rice pan. Put the lid back on and leave to stand off the heat. Stir in the mangetout when you are ready to serve.

5 Once the chicken is cooked, remove from the oven and slice. Spoon over the juices and serve.

Gruyère and Herb Salmon

4 medium **potatoes**, cut into 2cm chunks

oil

salt and **pepper**

4 **salmon** pieces

1 tablespoon freshly chopped **parsley**

1 tablespoon freshly chopped **basil**

½ mug grated **Gruyère** or **Cheddar cheese**

green beans

1 Preheat the oven to 180ºC fan oven/200ºC/gas 6.

2 Put the potatoes on a baking tray and sprinkle with the oil. Distribute well and season with salt and pepper. Place in the oven for 25–30 minutes.

3 After the potatoes have been in the oven for 25 minutes, heat a little oil in a frying pan. Add the salmon steaks, skin side down, and fry for 3 minutes on a medium heat.

4 Mix the parsley, basil and cheese. Sprinkle on the top of the steaks. Place under a hot grill for 5–6 minutes. Check to see that the salmon is cooked through; this, of course, depends on the thickness.

5 Serve with the potatoes and green beans.

Mini Meat Loaves

Tomato Sauce

oil to fry

1 **onion**, chopped

1 clove **garlic**, finely chopped

4 **tomatoes**, chopped

2 teaspoons **tomato purée** or **sun-dried tomato paste**

1 teaspoon **sugar**

salt and **pepper**

1 teaspoon **herbs** or 1 tablespoon freshly chopped **herbs**

1 **vegetable stock pot/cube (GF option)**

¼ mug **water**

Meat Loaves

500g **beef mince**

1 tablespoon chopped **fresh basil leaves**

1 clove **garlic**, crushed

1 **egg yolk**

2 x 125g balls of **mozzarella cheese**, chopped

1 tablespoon **olive oil**

200g pack of **streaky bacon**

new potatoes or **baked potatoes**

green beans or **sugar snaps**

1 Make the tomato sauce. Heat a little oil in a saucepan and fry the onions and garlic until they begin to soften. Add the rest of the ingredients and bring to the boil. Turn down to simmer for 10 minutes. Whizz with the blender.

2 Mix together the beef, basil, garlic and egg and season well.

3 Stir the chopped mozzarella into the mixture.

4 Spread the bacon slices on a large piece of cling film. Put the beef mixture on top and then roll the bacon around it to make one long sausage.

5 Unfold the cling film and cut in half.

6 Put the potatoes and greens on to boil.

7 Heat the oil in a large frying pan and fry the mini meat loaves on a low heat, for about 15 minutes. Turn frequently to make sure the bacon does not get too browned. Slice into 8 before serving (see photo).

8 Serve with the potatoes, sugar snaps and tomato sauce.

ALAN & JO: "Mini Meat loaves, what a great idea to have individual meat loaves. Delicious. We loved the tomato sauce, it would be great with pasta too."

Spiced Chicken & Herb Couscous

NOTE: This recipe works best when you use fresh herbs. They are so easy to keep in pots in the garden, or on a window sill (see "Nosh for Graduates" pages 8-11).

juice of ½ a **lemon**

1 teaspoon **cumin**

1 teaspoon **coriander**

½ teaspoon **paprika**

1 clove **garlic**, chopped finely

3 **chicken breasts**

1 mug **couscous**

grated zest of a **lemon**

1 **chicken stock pot/cube**

2 mugs boiling **water**

1 tablespoon **oil** to fry

1 **red onion**, chopped

1 **yellow pepper**, chopped

1 mug **couscous**

2 **tomatoes**, chopped

200g packet **feta cheese**, crumbled

1 tablespoon freshly chopped **basil**

1 tablespoon freshly chopped **coriander**

2 tablespoons **olive oil**

1   Mix together the lemon juice, cumin, coriander, paprika and garlic. Coat the chicken breasts and leave to stand for 5 minutes.

2   Put the couscous in a bowl with the lemon zest and stock. Add the boiling water. Put a plate over the bowl and leave to stand for 4 minutes. The water should be absorbed. If not, leave a little longer.

3   Heat a little oil in a frying pan and fry the onions and peppers until they begin to brown. Take out of the pan and set to one side.

4   Add a little more oil and fry the chicken breasts. Cook on a high heat for 2 minutes each side and then turn the heat down to medium. Pour the rest of the marinade into the pan. Put a lid or plate over the chicken breasts and cook each side for 4 minutes.

5   Meanwhile, add the onions and peppers,tomatoes, feta, herbs and olive oil to the couscous and mix well.

6   When the chicken breasts are cooked, cut them into strips and serve on top of the couscous.

ANDY & HEATHER: "We really like this dish. Nathan even requested it for his birthday dinner."

Mezze

12 Pitta Breads to Dip £0.43

When you have finished all the dips and pâtés, heat the pitta breads in a hot oven for 2-3 minutes. Whilst still warm, cut into dip-sized pieces.

Veg Sticks to Dip £2.73

1/2 **cucumber**, cut into strips

3 **carrots**, cut into strips

250g pack **baby sweetcorn**

1 **pepper**, cut into strips

4 sticks **celery**, cut into strips

Bean Dip £1.40

400g can **cannellini beans**

1 tablespoon **Greek yogurt**

10 **anchovy fillets**

juice of half a **lemon**

Blitz together.

Beetroot Salad £1.48

250g pack of **beetroot**, cut into small cubes

1/2 x 200g pack **feta**, crumbled

1 tablespoon **fresh basil**, chopped

1 tablespoon **olive oil**

Garlic Olives £0.73

Approx. 30 **olives, green and black**

1 tablespoon **olive oil**

1/2 clove **garlic**, finely chopped

1 tablespoon **freshly chopped basil and thyme**

salt and **pepper**

Just mix everything together.

Hollumi £2.15

250g pack of **Hollumi cheese**

olive oil to fry

salt and **pepper**

Cut the cheese into fairly thick slices. Fry quickly on a high heat. Season with salt and pepper.

Mackerel Pâté £2.96

4 small, **smoked mackerel fillets, ready-cooked**

2 large tablespoons **crème fraîche**

pepper

juice of 1/2 **lemon**

1 small clove **garlic**, chopped very finely

Mash everything together, or blitz very quickly in a food processor.

Pâté £1

200g pack of **duck or pork pâté**

Hummus £2.41

400g tin **chickpeas**

2 tablespoons **tahini paste**

1 clove **garlic**, chopped very finely

1 tablespoon **Greek yogurt**

1 teaspoon chopped **fresh basil**

juice of 1/2 **lemon**

1 **red pepper**, cut into chunks

1 tablespoon **oil**

salt and **pepper**

Heat the oil in a frying pan and fry the peppers on a medium heat for about 5 minutes, until they are browned and a bit soft. Using a hand-held blender or processor, blitz together the peppers, chickpeas, yogurt, tahini paste, lemon and peppers. Stir in the herbs and season well.

kids' parties

These times are such fun! You need to be around to enjoy them and not be in the kitchen all the time. The parties are designed so that everything can be made the day before. There is one party for 'littlies' and one for young teens.

kids' party food

Children love parties and they don't need to be really hard work for us. Here are a few helpful hints. Many of them obvious, which should make the time more fun for you. Enlist the help of a couple of the mums; they usually would rather help than stand around watching. Buy a piece of plastic tablecloth and sit them on the floor on cushions. This means they are closer together and gives a good atmosphere. Afterwards, you just need to wipe and sweep up. Have a few clean tea-towels handy, to quickly wipe up any spills or gunge. Steer clear of the foods containing additives and you will not have a room full of hyper children.

Keep things as simple as possible. Here are some food
suggestions. Just choose a few, don't try to do them all at once. Buy some chipolata sausages and twist them into tiny sausages. Roast them in the oven for 25 minutes and then cut them apart. Voila, mini sausages!

Veg sticks seem to go down well. Cut up some carrot,
celery and cucumber into sticks. Mix together a 200g pack of cream cheese and 1 dessertspoon of mango chutney. You could also add a few cherry tomatoes. Other finger food for them would be tiny cheese cubes, grapes and peeled satsumas.

Sandwiches are fairly staple. Cream cheese, ham, tuna and mayo
make good simple fillings. Cut them into shapes, if you have any cutters, otherwise, just cut off the crusts to make them more special. Eat the excess pieces to keep you going while you prepare.

Cakes and cookies are a must. Make "Butterfly Cakes" with big
chocolate buttons (page 228). Also, "Crispy Oat Cookies" (page 216) and "Coffee Shop Cookies" (page 220).

Rocky Roads (page 230) are good for older children. May be a bit much for
younger ones.

Birthday cakes. When it comes to birthday cakes, if you love making and
icing cakes, being up to your elbows in fondant and food colouring, then by all means make the cake. However, don't try to be a hero! There are some fabulous cakes you can buy at the supermarket. They may be fractionally more expensive than a home made one, but will save you loads of time and energy.

I love trifle! Most of the helpers and parents will also love it, together with
some of the kids. I've invented an almost healthy one called the "Jelly Berry Trifle" on page 236. It's full of fruit and not too sweet - give it a try.

To prevent spills. In order to prevent spills, it is wise to get some individual
packet drinks. Write each child's name on the box and, once they have wandered off, they can be reunited with their drink. You may see from the photos that we bought a really fun, inexpensive, pink tea set. No problem if it gets broken and I think it is going to be out on loan to a few people!

teens' movie night

There comes a time when the children do not really want us around at their party, be it a birthday, or just a get together with their friends. We discovered, however, that they would still like us to provide the food and the means for the party! We may be allowed to be there in the background, but certainly not too visible.

I asked a group of teenagers if they would like a video party. I gave them a certain amount of choice and this is what they decided on. They seem delighted to be fed, have the lounge to themselves for an evening, and to watch a video of their choice.

MENU

NACHOS

CHICKEN NUGGETS AND WEDGES
(RECIPE PAGE 180)

MILLIONAIRES SHORTBREAD
(RECIPE PAGE 218)

ROCKY ROADS
(RECIPE PAGE 230)

POPCORN
&
LOTS OF FIZZY DRINKS

getting kids involved

I started to cook when I was about 6 years old and this gave me lots of confidence when I later needed to be responsible in cooking for my family and friends. Getting kids involved with the preparation at any early age encourages their interest in cooking. I have included some fun recipes, which most kids will like. They are very simple and do-able for kids from about 3-18. One of my wonderful recipe testers, Jo, has three children and both she and her husband go out to work. As the children went through their teens, they had a family cooking-rota, so each week, everyone in the family would take a turn to cook the meal. I have to admit, I never managed to do this with my boys, but it is a great thing to aim for!

Spiced Apricot Turkey Burgers

NOTE: This one is really simple if you have a food processor. If you don't, it is a little more time consuming, but still worth it.

4 medium **potatoes**

oil

salt and **pepper**

4 **burger buns**

Burgers

1 large **onion,** chopped into quarters

2 cloves **garlic**

450g **turkey breast**

1 slice **wholemeal bread (GF option)**

4 **ready-to-eat apricots**

1 teaspoon **cumin**

1 teaspoon **coriander**

1/2 of a beaten **egg**

salt and **pepper**

1 Preheat the oven to 180ºC fan oven/200ºC/gas 6.

2 Cut the potatoes into wedges and place them on a roasting tray. Add the oil and salt and pepper and mix everything together with your hands. Place in the oven for 30 minutes.

3 If you do not have a food processor, finely chop up the burger ingredients and mix together.

4 If you have a processor, blitz the wholemeal bread first and place in a large bowl. Next, blitz the onion, garlic and apricots together. Add to the breadcrumbs.

5 Next, blitz the turkey breast; they will only need about 4–5 pulses as you don't want to make them into pulp. Mix this with the breadcrumbs and add the rest of the burger ingredients.

6 Form into 4–5 burger shapes. Make sure you press the mixture together well, so they don't fall apart when cooking.

7 Heat a little oil in a large frying pan and add the burgers. Fry on a medium heat for 10 minutes. The turkey should be cooked through in that time. Keep turning the burgers so they do not get too browned.

LUKE & RACH: "The apricots and turkey taste so great together! We often make these for the girls, but also for entertaining guests too. They're a winner with everyone. Luke would eat them every day if he could."

Beef Burgers with Crispy Fried Onions

¹/₂ **onion**, grated

500g **minced beef**

1 **egg yolk**

3 pieces of **sun-dried tomatoes**, finely chopped

salt and **pepper**

1 teaspoon **mustard (GF option)**

1 tablespoon **oil**

Crispy Fried Onions

1 large **onion**, sliced

1 dessertspoon **oil**

2cm cube **butter**

salt and **pepper**

4 **burger buns (GF option)**

1 Squeeze out any excess liquid from the onion. Mix with the rest of the ingredients for the burger. Using your hands, mix ingredients evenly until everything sticks together. Split into 4 and form into burgers.

2 Heat a tablespoon of oil in a large frying pan. Add the burgers, cook on a medium heat for 10–12 minutes. If you have made 5 burgers, it will take less time. Turn the burgers over every 3 minutes or so, to prevent them burning.

3 Meanwhile, to make the crispy fried onions, heat the oil and butter in a small frying pan and add the onions. Fry them on a medium heat until they become brown and crispy. This should take about the same length of time as the burgers will take to cook.

4 Serve together in a bread bun. Potato wedges go well (see page 19). If you put these in before you begin to prepare the burgers, everything should be ready about the same time.

Curried Lamb Burgers & Mango Salad

1 **onion**, grated

500g **lamb mince**

1 tablespoon **curry paste (GF option)** (mild or hot depending on taste)

1 **egg yolk**, beaten

serve with **salad** and/or **burger buns (GF option)**

Salad

2 **little gem lettuce**, sliced

4 **spring onions**, sliced

1 **mango**, stoned and sliced

1 **fat red chilli**, chopped

1 Squeeze the liquid from the grated onion and mix together with all the burger ingredients. Add just enough egg to make everything bind together, but not be too sloppy.

2 Form into burgers with your hands or by using a ring.

3 Heat a tablespoon of oil in a large frying pan and fry the burgers on a medium heat for 8–10 minutes, depending on how thick you have made them.

4 Serve with the salad, or in a bun.

Chicken Burgers

1 slice wholemeal **bread (GF option)**

½ **onion**

2 **chicken breasts,** each cut into 3

yoke of 1 **egg**

1 tablespoon freshly chopped **basil**

salt and **pepper**

serve in a **bun (GF option)** with **salad** and **mayo**

1. If you have a food processor, blitz the breadcrumbs and transfer them into a bowl. Chop the onion into quarters and blitz. Squeeze out the excess liquid. Add the chicken and pulse 4–5 times. Add to the breadcrumbs, along with the remaining burger ingredients and mix together.

2. If you do not have a food processor, finely chop the breadcrumbs and chicken breasts. Grate the onion and squeeze out any excess liquid. Mix together in a bowl with the remaining burger ingredients.

3. Form into burgers with your hands, or using a ring. Heat a little oil in a large frying pan and cook on a medium heat for 8–10 minutes, turning occasionally. Cut into the centre of one of the burgers to check they are cooked.

£ 1.68 /PERSON · SERVES 4 · EASE ★★☆☆☆ · PREP 20 MINS · COOK 25 MINS · OK TO FREEZE · GF OPTION

Super Simple Tuna Bake

2 mugs **pasta (GF option)**

1 mug **frozen peas**

2 x 185g tins **tuna**, drained

4 **spring onions**, chopped

300ml tub **soured cream**,

juice of ½ **lemon**

salt and **pepper**

1 mug grated **cheese**

2 small packets **ready-salted crisps**, crushed

1 Preheat the oven to 180ºC fan oven/200ºC/gas 6. Grease a large casserole dish.

2 Cook the pasta. Drain and add the frozen peas. Put the lid on the pan and leave to one side until needed.

3 Mix together the tuna, spring onions, soured cream and lemon juice. Add to the cooked pasta and peas and mix gently. Pour into the greased casserole dish.

4 Spread the crisps, then the cheese, over the top of the casserole dish.

5 Place in the oven for 20–25 minutes, until the crisps and cheese are browned.

Sausage and Chestnut Patties

NOTE: Use a food processor to make the patties and save time on all the chopping processes. You can freeze these when they are cold.

WHERE ON EARTH: You can buy cooked and peeled, whole chestnuts in Sainsburys. They are over the freezer counters, near the stock cubes.

3 medium **potatoes**, no need to peel

1 medium **butternut squash**

4 **tomatoes**, cut in ¼'s

1 tablespoon **oil**

Patties

500g pack **sausage meat**

2 slices of **wholemeal bread**, made into breadcrumbs

1 medium **onion**, chopped

6 medium **mushrooms**, chopped

1 teaspoon **mixed herbs**

200g pack **whole chestnuts** (cooked, peeled and ready to use), roughly chopped

salt and **pepper**

green veg

1 Preheat the oven to 180ºC fan oven/200ºC/ gas 6.

2 Cut the potatoes and butternut squash into 2cm cubes. Place on a baking tray with the tomatoes and drizzle with oil. Season with salt and pepper. Distribute the oil evenly, using your hands. Place in the oven for 50 minutes.

3 In a large bowl mix together the sausage meat, breadcrumbs, onions, mushrooms, herbs and chestnuts. Season well with salt and pepper. The mixture will be quite rustic. If you do this in a food processor, add things in the following order – onions, then mushrooms and chestnuts, then bread and finally sausage meat and herbs.

4 Form into 12 patties. Place on a greased baking tray and put in the oven for 40 minutes.

5 Serve with the roasted vegetables and cooked green veg or salad.

ANDY & HEATHER:
"These are good cold with some salad."

Watch a video of how to peal a squash at
noshbooks.com/squash

Wraps

Wraps are so quick and easy for children to make and are a good way into simple cooking. You can, of course, vary the ingredients. The recipes here just give an idea of the kinds of things to include. They work well with a bit of crunch (lettuce, cucumber, etc.), bit of sauce (hoisin, mayo, tomato sauce, BBQ or curry) and some meat. Chicken breast is easy to cook and it goes with so many different flavours.

BEN & NICOLE: "You could have so much fun doing these with kids and not get stressed at all. It's just like Bella putting her dolls in a blanket at bed-time...and then eating them. Maybe you could try using that example. Up to you!"

Cajun Chicken

£1.30 /PERSON

1 tablespoon **Cajun spice seasoning**

2 **chicken breasts**, cut into thin strips

oil to fry

4 **spring onions**, thinly sliced, lengthways

1 **red or yellow pepper**, thinly sliced

6 **corn tortillas**

1 **little gem lettuce**

4 tablespoons **soured cream**

1 Put the Cajun seasoning on a plate and dip the slices of chicken breast in. Cover evenly. Heat the oil in a frying pan and fry the chicken for 4–5 minutes, checking the thickest piece is thoroughly cooked.

2 Cut the chicken into thin strips.

3 Spread the mayo over each tortilla and divide the ingredients between them.

4 Roll up and cut each one in half and serve.

Chicken & Bacon

£1.41 /PERSON

8 slices **streaky bacon**

2 **chicken breasts**

4 tablespoons **mayo** or **soured cream**

8 **corn tortillas**

4 **spring onions**, sliced lengthways

1 **round lettuce**, washed and pulled apart

¼ **cucumber**, cut into strips

1 Fry the bacon until it is crispy. Set to one side.

2 Fry the chicken breasts for 2 minutes each side on a high heat. Turn the heat down and cook for 4 minutes each side, with a lid on the pan. Leave to stand for a couple of minutes and then cut into thin slices.

3 Spread the mayo on the tortillas and divide the ingredients evenly between them. Roll up and serve with the wedges.

Egg & Salmon

£0.95 /PERSON

6 **corn tortilla wraps**

2 tablespoons **mayo**

1 packet of **smoked salmon** (sandwich pack)

4 **hard-boiled eggs**, sliced

1 **little gem lettuce**

4 **spring onions**, thinly sliced lengthways

1 Spread each wrap with mayo.

2 Divide the salmon between the wraps and add the rest of the ingredients.

3 Roll each one up and cut in half and serve.

Chicken Quesadillas and Tomato Salsa

3 **chicken breasts**, cut into bite-sized strips

oil to fry

6 **mushrooms**, sliced

100g pack **spinach leaves**

6 small **corn tortillas**

1 mug grated **cheese**

guacamole (optional, depending on how old the children are and if they like spice)

Salsa

2 **tomatoes**, chopped

2 spring **onions**, chopped

1 tablespoon freshly chopped **basil**

juice of 1/2 **lemon**

dessertspoon **olive oil**

salt and **pepper**

1 Heat a little oil in a frying pan and fry the chicken until no longer pink. Add the mushrooms and fry for 30 seconds. Add the spinach and take the pan off the heat. The heat from the pan will cause the spinach to wilt.

2 Preheat the grill.

3 Spread the chicken, mushrooms and spinach evenly among the 6 tortillas. Sprinkle the cheese over and wrap them up (see photo). Place on a large baking tray. Brush the top of each one with a little oil.

4 Place under the grill for 2–3 minutes, or until the quesadilla is browned.

5 Mix the salsa ingredients together and serve with the quesadillas and guacamole.

BEN & NICOLE: "Who would have thought I'd like spinach? Turns out I do. This is why I love this book; it's opened my eyes to new food combos I wouldn't normally have tried."

One-Pot Sausage Meatballs

NOTE: You can stretch this to serve more people by adding another ½ mug of rice, 1 mug of water and more mushrooms.

500g pack of good quality **sausage meat**

1 tablespoon **oil**

1 **onion**, finely chopped

2 cloves **garlic**, finely chopped

6 **mushrooms**, sliced

1 mug **rice**

2 mugs **water**

1 **vegetable stock pot/cube**

400g tin chopped **tomatoes**

1 teaspoon **cumin**

1 teaspoon **ground coriander**

1 tablespoon **tomato purée**

2 tablespoons freshly chopped **coriander** (optional)

1 Cut the sausage meat into 16 and form balls from the portions. Heat the oil in a wok, or large pan, and fry on a medium heat until they are browned and cooked through. Take them out of the pan and set to one side until needed.

2 Add the onions and garlic to the pan and fry until the onions soften a little. Add the mushrooms and fry for 30 seconds.

3 Add the rice to the pan, along with the water, stock, tomatoes, cumin and coriander and tomato purée. Bring to the boil and then turn down to simmer, with a lid on, for 12–15 minutes. The rice should be tender, with a lot of the liquid absorbed.

4 Return the sausage balls to the pan and cook for 3–4 minutes.

5 Serve with the fresh coriander sprinkled over.

Chicken Nuggets and Wedges

NOTE: Kids love chicken nuggets. The problem is that they can cost a fortune and aren't going to be particularly healthy. This makes sure that you know exactly what they are eating and it won't break the bank.

4 large **potatoes**, cut into wedges

oil

salt and **pepper**

2 **eggs**

3 **slices bread (GF option)**, made into breadcrumbs

1 tablespoon **freshly chopped basil** or 1 teaspoon **dried basil**

1 mug finely grated **cheddar cheese**

3 **chicken breasts**, cut into strips, see photo

green veg, broccoli or **green beans**

tomato sauce or **mayo**, to serve

1   Preheat the oven to 200ºC fan oven/220ºC/ gas 7.

2   Put the potatoes on a baking tray. Sprinkle with oil and salt and pepper. Using your hands, distribute the oil evenly over the potatoes. Put in the oven for 25–30 minutes.

3   Beat the eggs and place in a bowl. Add 2 tablespoons flour to the bowl.

4   Mix together the breadcrumbs, basil and the cheese. Use a food processor if you have one.

5   Dip the pieces of chicken in the flour and the egg and then, one by one, in the breadcrumb mixture, coating each piece evenly. Place on a large, greased tray, leaving space between each one. Pile any extra breadcrumbs over the top of each one.

6   Place in the oven for 20 minutes. The chicken nuggets should be nicely browned.

7   While the chicken and potatoes are in the oven, put the greens on to cook.

LUKE & RACHEL: "Samantha and Melody are big fans of chicken nuggets and really love these! They were great finger food when Melody was being weaned and I know it was all good stuff in them for her."

budget days

End of the month, not much left in the piggy bank, so need to stretch things a little? Here we have some inexpensive meals that you and your family will enjoy.

Cumberland Hot Dogs with Tomato Salsa

6 large **Cumberland sausages (GF option)**

rolls (GF option)

lettuce leaves

soured cream, to serve

Tomato Salsa

oil to fry

4 **tomatoes**, chopped

½ fresh **red chilli**, deseeded and finely chopped

1 clove **garlic**, finely chopped

1 tablespoon fresh **basil**, chopped or 1 teaspoon **freeze-dried basil**

1 teaspoon **sugar**

1 tablespoon **tomato purée**

1 tablespoon **red wine vinegar**

salt and **pepper**

1 Preheat the oven to 180ºC fan oven/200ºC/ gas 6. Place the sausages on a tray in the oven and cook for 25 minutes, or until brown.

2 Meanwhile, make the salsa. Heat a little oil in a frying pan and add the tomatoes, chilli and garlic. Fry for 1 minute to heat through. Add the rest of the salsa ingredients and heat through. Leave to cool.

3 Cut the long rolls almost in half, add the sausage and serve with the salsa and the soured cream.

Masala Mince

1 **onion**, sliced

1 clove **garlic**, finely chopped

1 fat **red chilli**, chopped (less if you have young children)

1 tablespoon freshly grated **ginger**

500g **minced beef**

400g tin **tomatoes**

1 tablespoon **tomato purée**

1 **beef stock pot/cube (GF option)**

salt and **pepper**

2 teaspoons **garam masala**

2 tablespoons **freshly chopped corinader**

rice with pilau seasoning (see page 16)

1 Heat a little oil in a large saucepan or wok. Add the onions and garlic, chilli and ginger. Fry until the onions begin to soften.

2 Add the mince and fry until no longer pink.

3 Add the rest of the ingredients. Bring to the boil and then turn down to simmer for 20 minutes.

4 After 10 minutes, put the rice on to cook (see page 16). After another 5 minutes, put the green beans on to cook.

5 Serve with the cooked rice, coriander andgreen beans and mango chutney.

£ 1.27 /PERSON | SERVES 4 | EASE ★★★☆☆ | PREP 30 MINS | V

Courgette Fritters with Feta Salad

Salad Dressing

juice of a **lemon**

1 tablespoon **olive oil**

1 teaspoon **sugar**

salt and **pepper**

Feta and Tomato Salad

1 little gem **lettuce**

8cm **cucumber**, cut into sticks

2 **spring onions** cut into thin strips

6-8 **cherry tomatoes,** halved

1 tablespoon **pine nuts**

200g **feta cheese**, crumbled

Fritters

4 **eggs**

1 mug **self-raising flour**

salt and **pepper**

3 **courgettes**, grated

2 **spring onions** or 1 small **onion**, grated

1/2 x 400g tin **sweetcorn**, drained

salt and **pepper**

1 Mix the salad dressing ingredients together.

2 Put the eggs in a bowl and beat together with the flour and salt and pepper.

3 Squeeze out any excess liquid from the grated onion and courgettes. Add to the egg mixture along with the sweetcorn. Season well.

4 Heat a little oil in a frying pan and add 1 tablespoon of the fritter mix. You can cook 3 or 4 at a time. Continue until all the fritter mix is used up.

5 Sprinkle the dressing over the salad and serve with the fritters.

PETER & BERNICE: "The feta, pine nuts and the quick and simple dressing gives the salad a fresh, tangy flavour and great texture. Hot fritters and cold salad works surprisingly well together, and the whole meal looks really tempting

One-Pot Chicken Hot Pot

NOTE: If you have one, use a food processor for the potato slices.

oil to fry

1 **onion**, sliced

2 cloves **garlic**, chopped

8 boneless **chicken thighs**, cut into bite-sized pieces

1 tablespoon **flour**

4 **carrots**, diced

2 sweet **potatoes**, peeled and cubed

1 mug **frozen peas**

1 teaspoon **mixed dried herbs**

1 **chicken stock pot/cube**

1 tablespoon **HP sauce**

1½ mugs **water**

4 large **potatoes**, cut into ½cm slices

1 Preheat the oven to 180ºC fan oven/200ºC/ gas 6.

2 Heat a little oil in a large hob-to-oven casserole dish. Add the onion and garlic and fry until the onion begins to soften.

3 Add the chicken and cook until no longer pink. Sprinkle over with flour and mix.

4 Add the carrots, sweet potato, peas, mixed herbs, stock, HP sauce and water. Bring to the boil. Season well.

5 Take off the heat and arrange the sliced potatoes over the top of the chicken mix. Season well.

6 Put a lid on the casserole and place in the oven for 30 minutes. Take the lid off and cook for a further 30 minutes, or until the potatoes are browned.

£ 0.87 /PERSON SERVES 4 EASE ★★★☆☆ PREP 30 MINS GF

Corned Beef Hash with Poached Eggs

NOTE: Leaving the hash to brown on the pan is vital to getting lots of flavour from all the crunchy bits.

4 large **potatoes**, cut into 2cm cubes

1 tablespoon **oil**

1 **onion**, sliced

1 **yellow pepper**, chopped

350g tin **corned beef**, cut into cubes

1 teaspoon **paprika**

4 **eggs**

1 tablespoon freshly chopped **parsley**

salt and **pepper**

1 Put the potatoes in boiling water and simmer for 10 minutes. Drain and return to the pan.

2 Heat the oil and butter in a wok and fry the onions and peppers, until they begin to brown. Add the paprika and season well with salt and pepper.

3 Add the potatoes and corned beef to the pan. Leave to fry for 2 minutes, until the stuff on the bottom begins to brown. Stir up the brown bits, then leave for another 2 minutes. Stir up the brown bits from the bottom. Don't keep stirring all the time, allow things to brown.

4 Poach the eggs (see video link below).

5 Serve the eggs on top of the hash and sprinkle with the parsley.

Watch a video of poaching eggs at
noshbooks.com/poaching-eggs

Crispy Topped Vegetable Bake

1 **red onion**, chopped

1 **red pepper**, chopped

1 clove **garlic**, finely chopped

2 tablespoons **Worcestershire sauce**

1 mug **rice**, cooked with 2 mugs of **water** (see page 16)

8 **mushrooms**, sliced

4 large **tomatoes**, chopped

2 slices **wholemeal bread**, made into breadcrumbs

1 teaspoon dried **mixed herbs** or 1 tablespoon freshly chopped **basil**

1 mug grated **Cheddar cheese**

salt and **pepper**

4 **eggs**

1   Preheat the oven to 180ºC fan oven/200ºC/ gas 6. Grease a large casserole dish.

2   Heat a little oil in a wok and fry the onion, peppers and garlic. Once browned, add the Worcestershire sauce and mix together.

3   Add the cooked rice, mushrooms and tomatoes to the wok. Season well with salt and pepper and mix gently. Place in the casserole dish.

4   Make 4 hollows in the rice and break an egg into each one.

5   Mix together the breadcrumbs, herbs and cheese. Sprinkle over the top and place in the oven for 30 minutes. The top should be browned a little. If your children are older, you can replace the Cheddar with Parmesan.

Smoked Salmon and Cream Cheese Spaghetti

spaghetti (see page 17)

2 medium **courgettes**, thinly sliced

1 tablespoon **olive oil**

6 **spring onions**, chopped

200g pack of **smoked salmon trimmings**

300ml pack of **cream cheese with garlic and herbs**

zest and juice of a **lemon**

1. Put the spaghetti on to boil and simmer for 5–6 minutes.

2. Heat the oil in a wok and add the courgettes. Fry for 1-2 minutes until they begin to soften.

3. Add the onions, salmon and cream cheese to the pan and cook until everything is heated through. This will take 2 minutes max. Add the lemon juice and zest.

4. Drain the spaghetti, but retain the cooking liquid.

5. Add the spaghetti to the wok along with a little of the spaghetti water. Mix together.

6. Serve straight away.

Beef and Mushroom Pie with Crispy Potato Top

NOTE: Ovens vary slightly, so make sure you leave this in the oven until the potatoes are nice and crispy on top.

2 tablespoons **olive oil**

1 **onion**, roughly chopped

1 clove **garlic**, finely chopped

500g **beef mince**

1 tablespoon **flour (GF option)**

400g tin **chopped tomatoes**

250g pack **mushrooms**, sliced

1 tablespoon **tomato purée**

1 teaspoon **sugar**

1 teaspoon **dried mixed herbs**

1 mug **water**

1 **beef stock pot/cube (GF option)**

3–4 medium **potatoes**

1   Preheat the oven to 180ºC fan oven/200ºC/gas 6.

2   Heat 1 tablespoon of the oil in a frying pan and fry the onion and garlic for 2 minutes.

3   Add the mince and cook until no longer pink.

4   Add the flour and stir well.

5   Add the tomatoes, mushrooms, tomato purée, sugar, herbs, water and liquid stock. Bring to the boil for the sauce to thicken. Leave to simmer for 10 minutes.

6   If you have a food processor, grate the potatoes on the most coarse setting, or just use the coarse setting on a cheese grater. No need to peel the potatoes. Squeeze out the excess liquid from the potatoes, place in a large bowl and add the other tablespoon of oil, together with plenty of salt and pepper. Mix together.

7   Put the mince mixture into the casserole dish and spread the potatoes over the top, as loosely as you can, as the heat needs to get to them all. Place in the oven for 35–40 minutes, until the potatoes are cooked and browned on top.

BEN & NICOLE: "If you have a food processor, doing the potato top is so quick. It makes a delicious crunchy crust."

£1.00 /PERSON | SERVES **4** | EASE ★★☆☆☆ | PREP 25 MINS | COOK 50 MINS | OK TO FREEZE ❄ | GF OPTION

Sausage and Veg Traybake

NOTE: You can also add carrots, courgettes or tomatoes to the roast veg. This is a good way to use up the veg left in the fridge at the end of the week.

ONE MORE THING: Also can add ½ teaspoon paprika to the tomato sauce to spice it up, if you like.

WHERE ON EARTH: White wine vinegar is usually near the frozen section, with the 'regular' vinegars.

8–12 fat **sausages (GF option)**

4 medium **potatoes**, cut into 3cm chunks

1 **red onion**, cut into wedges

2 **parsnips**, cut into long strips

2 **sweet potatoes**, cut into 2cm chunks

olive oil

salt and **pepper**

sprig of fresh **rosemary**, or 1 teaspoon **dried rosemary**

Piquant Tomato Sauce

oil to fry

1 **onion**, sliced

400g tin **tomatoes**

1 teaspoon **black pepper**

1 tablespoon **tomato purée**

1 tablespoon **white wine vinegar**

1 teaspoon **sugar**

1 Preheat the oven to 180ºC fan oven/200ºC/gas 6.

2 Put the sausages and vegetables into a roasting tray, sprinkle well with oil and distribute it with your hands. Season well with salt and pepper and sprinkle some rosemary over the top. Put in the oven for 45–50 minutes.

3 While everything is roasting, make the tomato sauce. Heat the oil in a saucepan, add the onions and fry until soft. Add the rest of the ingredients and bring to the boil. Simmer for 2–3 minutes. Blitz with a hand-held blender.

LUKE & RACHEL: "Very easy. I love meals you can prepare during nap times and put in the oven when you want."

Oriental Egg and Smoked Salmon Bake

NOTE: Smoked salmon has quite a strong taste, so the small quantity here will provide enough flavour. The trimmings are very economical and can be frozen, so it's really handy to keep some in the freezer.

1 mug **rice**, cooked in 2 mugs water

200g pack of **smoked salmon trimmings**

6 **spring onions**, chopped

salt and **pepper**

1 tablespoon **sesame oil** or toasted sesame oil

2 tablespoons **soy sauce (GF option)**

6 **eggs**, beaten

½ x 300ml pot **soured cream**

1 mug grated **cheese**

salad to serve

1 Preheat the oven to 200ºC fan oven/220ºC/gas 7. Grease a shallow casserole dish.

2 Cook the rice (see page 16). Pour the rice into the casserole dish.

3 Add the salmon and spring onions and distribute evenly. Season well with salt and pepper.

4 Add the sesame oil and soy to the beaten eggs and gently stir. Pour into the casserole dish.

5 Spoon the soured cream over the top and then sprinkle the cheese over.

6 Place in the oven for 15–20 minutes until the cheese bubbles and begins to go brown.

7 Serve with salad.

DAVID & HANNAH: "This would not be a recipe I'd normally choose myself, but I was surprised how tasty it was. I loved that it was so easy to make and good value. I will do it again."

£0.70 /PERSON · SERVES 4 · EASE ★★★☆☆ · PREP 30 MINS · COOK 25 MINS · OK TO FREEZE · V GF OPTION

Cheese and Onion Patties with Apple Chutney

4 medium **potatoes,** cut into small cubes

oil

5 slices of **wholemeal bread (GF option),** made into breadcrumbs

1³/₄ mugs grated **Cheddar cheese**

3 **spring onions,** chopped

2 sprigs of fresh **thyme,** leaves only

1 tablespoon chopped **fresh parsley**

3 **eggs**

salt and **pepper**

Apple Chutney

oil to fry

1 **onion,** chopped

1 eating **apple,** cored and chopped

1 tablespoon **soy sauce (GF option)**

1 tablespoon **wine vinegar**

1¹/₂ tablespoons **honey**

2 tablespoons **water**

1 Preheat the oven to 180ºC fan oven/200ºC/gas 6.

2 Put the potatoes on a baking tray, sprinkle with oil, season well and distribute well with your hands. Put in the oven for 30–35 minutes.

3 Mix together the breadcrumbs, cheese, spring onions, thyme and parsley.

4 Add 2 eggs and one egg yolk. Season well and mix together.

5 Turn out onto a board and form 8 small patties. Place on a greased baking tray and put in the oven, with the potatoes, for 20 minutes.

6 To make the chutney, put a little oil in a saucepan and fry the onions, until they begin to brown a little. Add the rest of the ingredients and simmer gently for 5 minutes. Set to one side until needed.

7 Serve the patties with the mini roasts and the chutney.

PETER & BERNICE: "This quick meal is bursting with a variety of textures and flavours. The patties are crunchy on the outside and soft on the inside and the tangy apple chutney is a great flavour contrast. Mini roasts taste much better than chips, and are healthier as you leave the skins on and you don't need lots of oil to cook them. We have thyme growing in our garden, and usually the other ingredients are to hand, so this is a brilliant recipe for those "arrgh, nothing planned for tea" moments. Guaranteed clean plates all round."

Sausage Stew with Borlotti Beans

NOTE: Try experimenting with different flavoured sausages to change the taste.

1 tablespoon **oil**

8 thick **sausages**

1 **onion**, sliced

1 clove **garlic**, chopped

4 **tomatoes**, chopped

1 tablespoon **tomato purée**

1 **vegetable stock pot/cube**

2 mugs **water**

1 teaspoon **mixed herbs**

1 pinch **chilli flakes**

1 portion of **spaghetti**, broken into pieces

400g tin **borlotti beans**, drained and rinsed

1 Heat a little oil in a wok and fry the sausages until they are browned on the outside and cooked through. Take out of the pan and leave to one side until needed.

2 Add the onions and garlic to the wok and fry until the onions begin to soften.

3 Add the tomatoes and fry for 1 minute.

4 Add the tomato purée, stock, water, herbs, chilli and the broken spaghetti. Cut each sausage into 4 and return to the pan. Bring to the boil and then turn down to simmer, with the lid on, for 4–5 minutes, or until the spaghetti is cooked. Add more water if necessary.

5 Add the beans and cook for 1 minute, or until the beans are heated through.

DAVID & HANNAH: "This was very easy and quick to make, the kids and I really enjoyed it. I like the little kick the chilli flakes give it."

Pastitsio

NOTE: If you have a food processor, use it for the breadcrumbs and then change the attachment and grate the cheese straight in. Very quick, no fuss.

1 tablespoon **oil**

1 **onion**, chopped

2 cloves **garlic, chopped**

500g **minced beef**

400g tin chopped **tomatoes**

1 tablespoon **tomato purée**

1 **beef stock pot/cube**

2 mugs **pasta**

2 heaped tablespoons **flour**

50g **butter** (measure using packet)

2 mugs **milk**

2 slices **wholemeal bread**, made into breadcrumbs

1 mug grated **cheese**

1 tablespoon freshly chopped **basil,** or 1 teaspoon **dried basil**

salt and **pepper**

1 Heat the oil in a wok or large pan and fry the onion and garlic until it begins to brown.

2 Add the meat to the pan and fry until it is no longer pink.

3 Add the tomatoes, tomato purée and stock. Bring to the boil, then turn down to simmer for 10 minutes. Season well with salt and pepper

4 Put the pasta on to cook (see page 17). Drain and leave until needed.

5 Heat the oven to 180ºC fan oven/200ºC/gas 6. Grease a casserole dish.

6 Make the sauce by putting the flour and butter in a pan. Heat and stir until it forms a paste. Gradually stir in, or whisk the milk, until you have a creamy consistency. Gently bring to the boil and cook for 30 seconds. Season well with salt and pepper.

7 Put the pasta on the bottom of the casserole dish, press down. Pour the meat sauce over and spread. Pour the white sauce over the top.

8 Mix together the breadcrumbs, basil and grated cheese and sprinkle over the top. Place in the oven for 20–25 minutes until the top is browned and crispy.

JOE & SARAH: "Joe's parents own an Italian Deli, so we eat pasta quite often, but I have never cooked pasta as a bake. I invited the family over the day I tried this and it was pleasing to see all the plates mopped up and squeaky clean. Yippee, less washing up for me!"

cakes & cookies

We all need a treat every now and then. Some of these cakes and cookies are downright naughty, whilst others have a hint of 'healthy' about them. Heather, another of my amazing testers, made the "Apricot Flap Jacks" and convinced herself that they must be good for her as they had oats, seeds and dried fruit in them, despite the syrup and sugar. Her imagination could not convince her of the same when it came to test the 'Millionaire's Shortbread'! Both went down really well with her family. There are some lunch-box cookies which will work out much cheaper than cereal bars.

Date and Nut Bars

½ mug/105g **brown sugar**

½ mug/85g **self-raising flour**

½mug/60g **oats**

1 teaspoon **mixed spice**

250g **ready-to-eat dates**, chopped

½ x 200g packet **pecans** or other nuts, chopped

2 **eggs**

⅓ mug/100ml vegetable **oil**

1   Preheat the oven to 160ºC fan oven/180ºC/gas 5. Grease and line a 20x30cm baking tray.

2   Mix the dry ingredients together in a bowl.

3   Beat the eggs, mix in the oil and add to the dry ingredients. Mix well.

4   Press into the baking tray and place in the oven for 25 minutes.

5   Leave to cool and cut into approx. 18 pieces.

STEVE & CANDY: "I love the fact that it has got mug measures. I really enjoy the mixed spice flavour."

£ 2.61 /TOTAL · MAKES 20 · EASE ★★☆☆☆ · PREP 20 MINS · COOK 12 MINS · OK TO FREEZE · V

Orange Cookies

180g softened **butter** (measure using packet)

½ mug/135g **sugar**

2 **egg** yolks

1 teaspoon **vanilla extract**

grated zest of an **orange**

1½ mugs/230g **self-raising flour**

Topping

1 mug/185g **icing sugar**

juice of an **orange**

sprinkles

1 Preheat the oven to 180ºC fan oven/200ºC/gas 6. Grease 2 baking trays.

2 Cream the butter and sugar together. Add the egg yolks and the vanilla. Mix well.

3 Stir in the orange zest and then the flour. Mix to a stiff dough.

4 Make about 20 small balls and place them on the trays. Give them a squash down.

5 Place in the oven for 12 minutes until slightly browned.

6 Once cooled, mix the icing sugar and enough orange juice together to make a fairly stiff icing. Put a blob on each cookie and then shake over with a few sprinkles.

Carrot Cake Tray Bake

NOTE: You can make this recipe into small buns, it makes about 24. Put in bun cases and bake in the oven for 25 minutes. Makes good lunch box additions.

4 **eggs**

1 mug/210g **soft brown sugar**

²/₃ mug/165ml **sunflower oil**

2 mugs/340g **self-raising flour**

1¹/₂ teaspoon ground **cinnamon**

4 medium **carrots**, grated

zest and juice of an **orange**

Topping

300g pack of **soft cream cheese** (Philadelphia)

50g **butter** (measure using packet)

²/₃ mug/125g **icing sugar**

1 teaspoon grated **orange rind**

1 Preheat the oven to 160ºC fan oven/180ºC/gas 4. Grease and line a 20x30cm cake tin.

2 Separate the eggs and beat the whites to a soft peak.

3 In a separate bowl, whisk the egg yolks together with the sugar until they go pale.

4 Gradually add the oil, whisking all the time.

5 Add the flour, cinnamon, carrots, zest and juice of the orange. Mix gently together.

6 Gently add the egg whites and mix well.

7 Pour into the cake tin and bake in the oven for 40–45 minutes.

8 To make the topping simply mix the ingredients together and leave in the fridge until needed. Do not over mix, as the cream cheese will go runny.

9 Once the cake is cooled, spread the topping over.

GARY & NIKKI: "This is the best carrot cake I have ever tried. The family gave it 10/10."

Banana and Pecan Nut Cake

150g softened **butter** (measure using packet)

²/₃ mug/140g **soft brown sugar**

2 **eggs**

3 ripe **bananas**, crushed

¹/₂ mug/50g **pecan nuts**, chopped roughly

¹/₃ mug/125g **raisins**

1²/₃ mugs/280g **self-raising flour**

Topping

2 tablespoons **marmalade**

¹/₂ x100g packet **flaked almonds**

1 Preheat the oven to 180ºC fan oven/200ºC/ gas 6. Grease and line a 20x30cm baking tray.

2 Cream the butter and sugar until soft and creamy.

3 Add the eggs, one at a time, together with the bananas, and beat well.

4 Add the chopped nuts, raisins and flour. Fold in until well mixed, but do not beat.

5 Pour into the cake tin and spread evenly. Place in the oven for 35–40 minutes. The cake should be nicely browned and bounce back when pressed.

6 Gently heat the marmalade in a pan. Brush over the top of the warm cake. Sprinkle with the almonds.

Lunch Box Cookies

250g **butter**, softened

¾ mug/170g **brown sugar**

2 **eggs**

1 mug/170g **self-raising flour**

1½ mugs/185g **rolled oats**

⅓ mug/50g **raisins**

½ mug/50g **desiccated coconut**

1 mug/200g **ready-to-eat apricots**, chopped finely

1 Preheat the oven to 180ºC fan oven/200ºC/gas 6.

2 Beat the butter and sugar until light and fluffy.

3 Add the eggs, one at a time, and beat again.

4 Add the rest of the ingredients and mix.

5 Place dessertspoons of the dough on greased baking trays and flatten down a little. Place in the oven for 12–15 minutes, until they are golden brown. They will still be a little soft in the centre. If you want more crispy biscuits, leave them in the oven for another 5 minutes.

£2.72 /TOTAL MAKES 20 EASE ★★☆☆☆ PREP 25 MINS COOK 10 MINS OK TO FREEZE ❄ V

Chocolate Oat Cookies

225g **butter** (measure using packet), melted

1 rounded tablespoon **golden syrup**

1¹/₂ mugs/185g **oats**

¹/₂ mug/135g **sugar**

1 mug/170g **self-raising flour**

¹/₂ x 100g pack of **chocolate chips**

100g melted **chocolate** to decorate

1 Preheat the oven to 180ºC fan oven/200ºC/gas 6. Grease 2 large baking trays.

2 Melt the butter and syrup in a pan.

3 Put the oats, sugar, flour and chocolate chips in a large bowl and mix together. Add the butter and syrup and mix well.

4 Place dessertspoons of the mixture on the trays, but set well apart, as they will spread to about 8cm. Press down the centres.

5 Place in the oven for 8–10 minutes, until they just begin to brown on the outsides. The centres will still appear a bit soft.

6 Once cooled, drizzle over the melted chocolate.

BEN & NICOLE:
"Really easy. The kids loved them. I even overcooked them and they were still great."

Millionaire's Shortbread

NOTE: Scoring the chocolate, when it is half-set, stops it cracking when you come to cut the cookies at the end.

Base

200g **butter** (measure using packet)

1/3 mug/80g **caster sugar**

1¾ mugs/300g **plain flour**

Centre

50g **butter** (measure by packet)

1/3 mug/90g **granulated sugar**

400g tin **condensed milk**

2 tablespoons **golden syrup**

Topping

200g bar **milk chocolate**

100g bar **white chocolate** (optional for extra decoration)

1 Preheat the oven to 180ºC fan oven/200ºC/gas 6. Grease and line a baking tray.

2 Cream the butter and sugar. Add the flour and mix together. Press into the baking tray and place in the oven for 12–15 minutes.

3 Put the butter, sugar, condensed milk and syrup in the saucepan and gently heat. Bring to the boil and stir frequently. Allow to simmer gently for 5–8 minutes until it turns golden brown. Leave to cool for 5 minutes and then pour over the shortbread. Leave to set for about 1 hour.

4 Melt the chocolate in a bowl over a pan of simmering water.

5 Spread the chocolate over the caramel and leave in the fridge for 45 mins. Score the top of the chocolate, as if you were going to cut it.

6 Leave in the fridge until the chocolate has completely set. Cut into squares and hide it from any chocoholics!

ANDY & HEATHER:
"Absolutely yummy, the family loved these."

Watch a video of how to do feathering at
noshbooks.com/feathering

Coffee Shop Cookies

NOTE: This is a good one to do with small children. One good way to soften butter is to let the child squish the butter with their freshly washed hands. Works wonders and they love it.

ONE MORE THING: Try playing around with the oven timing to get the perfect cookie, as all ovens vary a little.

100g **butter** (measure using packet)

1¼ mugs/260g **soft brown sugar**

½ x 375g pot of **Nutella**

1 teaspoon **vanilla extract**

1 **egg**

1 mug/170g **self-raising flour**

1 tablespoon **cocoa**

½ x 100g packet **chocolate chips**

½ mug **pecans**, chopped

white chocolate to decorate

1 Preheat the oven to 180ºC fan oven/200ºC/gas 6. Grease or line a couple of baking trays.

2 Cream together the butter and sugar.

3 Add the Nutella, vanilla and the egg and beat well.

4 Add the flour, cocoa, chocolate chips and the pecans. Mix well.

5 Put dessertspoons of the mixture well apart on the trays. They will spread quite a lot and make quite thin cookies.

6 Bake for 12 minutes in the oven. They will look as though they are not cooked, but when left to cool, will be crunchy on the outside and chewy in the centre.

7 Once cooled, drizzle with a bit of melted white chocolate.

JOE & SARAH: "These are delicious. They did not even last the day before they were gone."

Watch a video of how to melt chocolate at
noshbooks.com/melting-chocolate

Melting Moments

175g **butter** (measure using packet), softened

⅓ mug/60g **icing sugar**

1 mug/200g **plain flour**

½ mug/60g **cornflour**

1 teaspoon **vanilla extract**

Filling

125g **butter** (measure using packet), softened

1 mug/185g **icing sugar**

1 teaspoon **vanilla extract**

1 Heat the oven to 160ºC fan oven/180ºC/gas 4. Grease a baking tray.

2 Beat the butter and icing sugar together.

3 Add the flour, cornflour and vanilla extract and beat, until the mixture holds together.

4 Flour a board and cut into 32 pieces. Roll into balls and place on the baking tray. They will not spread too much, so can be fairly close together. Press a fork onto the tops of the dough balls and squash down a little. This makes a pretty mark.

5 Place in the oven for 10–12 minutes, until very slightly browned. Leave to cool.

6 Make the filling by beating the ingredients together. Once the cookies are cooled, sandwich them together with the filling. Dust the tops with icing sugar.

Apricot Flap Jacks

125g **butter** (measure using packet)

½ mug/105g **soft brown sugar**

3 rounded tablespoons **golden syrup**

2 mugs/240g **rolled oats (GF option)**

½ x 100g packet of **pumpkin seeds** or **mixed seeds**

½ mug or 12 **ready-to-eat-apricots**, chopped

1 Heat the oven to 160ºC fan oven/180ºC/gas 4. Line a 20x30cm baking tray.

2 Put the butter, sugar and syrup in a saucepan and gently heat, until everything is melted and the sugar dissolved.

3 Put the oats, seeds and apricots in a large bowl. Stir in the syrup mixture and mix until you cannot see any dry oats.

4 Press into the baking tray and flatten out with a palette knife. Place in the oven for 20–25 minutes. The top should be browned a little.

5 Leave to cool and cut into bars. This should make good lunch box fillers.

Chocolate Chip Cookies

NOTE: Don't skimp on the butter and use margarine instead, it won't taste nearly as good!

ONE MORE THING: You can freeze the mixture, so that you can defrost and cook at a later date.

125g softened **butter** (measure using packet)

1 mug/210g **soft brown sugar**

1 large **egg**

1 teaspoon of **vanilla** extract

100g packet **white chocolate chips**

1½ mugs/225g **self-raising flour**. Take out 1 tablespoon and replace with 1 tablespoon **cocoa**

1 Preheat the oven to 180ºC fan oven/200ºC/gas 6. Grease 2 baking trays.

2 Mix the butter and sugar together and beat well. Add the egg and the vanilla extract. Beat well.

3 Add the chocolate chips and mix, then add the flour and mix well. The cookie dough will be quite stiff. Tip onto a floured surface and squash into a long sausage. Do not knead the dough; in fact, handle it as little as possible. Cut into 16 and roll each portion into a ball. Squash each ball until it is about 1.5cm thick and approximately 6cm across. Place on the baking tray.

4 Put in the oven and bake for 10–12 minutes. The cookies do not need to brown, just be crisp on the outside. Leave to cool for a few minutes.

DAVID & HANNAH: "These cookies are great and very easy to do with the kids. Very quick and not too messy! My girls had one in their school lunch boxes and thought they were yummy."

224

£0.80 /TOTAL · MAKES 12 · EASE ★☆☆☆☆ · PREP 20 MINS · COOK 20 MINS · OK TO FREEZE · V

Muffins

3 mugs/525g **self-raising flour**

1 mug/175g **brown or white sugar**

2 **eggs**, slightly beaten

1½ mugs **milk**

¾ mug **vegetable oil**

muffin cases

1 Preheat oven to 180ºC fan oven/200ºC/gas 6.

2 Mix all the dry ingredients together, then add the 'wet ones'. It will be a bit lumpy and quite 'wet'.

3 Fill 18 large muffin cases and bake in the oven for 25 minutes. If you use smaller bun cases, you will only need to bake them for 20 minutes.

Variations

Chocolate chip muffins

Add two 100g packets of chocolate chips. Two different varieties work well; for example, white and milk chocolate. If you want double choc chip muffins, instead of the 3 mugs of flour, use 2²/₃ flour and ¹/₃ mug drinking chocolate.

Raspberry or blueberry muffins

Take ³/₄ x 400g bag of defrosted frozen fruit, drain away the liquid and add the fruit to the wet ingredients.

Apple cinnamon muffins

Add 1 mug of finely chopped apple to the wet ingredients and 2 teaspoons ground cinnamon to the dry ingredients.

Banana and nut muffins

Add 1 mug of mashed, ripe banana and 1 mug of chopped nuts (cashews, Brazils, pecans or walnuts) along with the wet ingredients.

Chocolate and maple muffins

Add ½ mug maple syrup to the wet ingredients and 200g chocolate (white or milk), chopped into chunks, to the dry ingredients.

Butterfly Cakes

NOTE: If you wish, you can add colouring to the icing and put sprinkles on the top. If you want to make chocolate cakes, replace a tablespoon of the four with a tablespoon of cocoa and add ½ teaspoon baking powder.

ONE MORE THING: These are great for kids' parties.

170g softened **butter** (measure using packet)

²/₃ mug/160g **caster sugar**

3 **eggs**

1 teaspoon **vanilla extract**

1 mug/170g **self-raising flour**

12 **bun cases**

Filling

100g softened **butter** (measure using packet)

1 mug/185g **icing sugar**

1 Preheat the oven to 180°C fan oven/200°C/gas 6. Put the bun cases in the bun tins.

2 Beat the sugar and butter until smooth. To make life easier, use a food mixer or processor.

3 Add the eggs, one at a time, and the vanilla extract. Beat until light in colour.

4 Gently fold in the flour, but don't over mix. If the eggs were small, add a tablespoon of water to the mix. Place a heaped dessertspoon in each bun case. Should make 12 cakes.

5 Put in the oven for 15–20 minutes. The cakes should have risen and be golden brown.

6 To make the filling, beat the butter and the icing sugar together.

7 Once the cakes are cooled, cut out a circle from the top of each cake and cut that circle in half. Put about a dessertspoon of the butter cream in each cake and place the two halves of the circle to form wings (see photo).

8 Put a tablespoon of icing sugar in a sieve and shake over the cakes.

BEN & NICOLE: "These are suprisingly easy to make and taste fab. The kids love the way they look."

£5.87 /TOTAL | MAKES 24 | EASE ★★★☆☆ | PREP 20 MINS | COOL 2 HOURS ❄ | OK TO FREEZE ❄ | V

Rocky Road

NOTE: Cut these very small as they are quite rich. They make great treats for a kids' party.

100g **butter** (measured using the packet)

225g **plain chocolate**

2 tablespoons **golden syrup**

2 tablespoons **caster sugar**

1 tablespoon **cocoa powder**

100g packet **Maltesers**

100g packet of **white chocolate chips**

100g packet **mini marshmallows**

¾ x 300g packet of **Hobnobs**, broken up

icing sugar

1 Line a baking tray with greaseproof paper.

2 Gently heat the butter, chocolate, syrup and sugar in a pan, until the sugar crystals disappear. Stir in the cocoa powder and mix until smooth. Leave to cool for 15 minutes.

3 Put the Maltesers, chocolate chips, marshmallows and biscuits in a large mixing-bowl. Once the chocolate has cooled, pour into the bowl and mix everything together.

4 Tip into the baking tray and spread evenly. Place in the fridge for at least 2 hours. Turn out onto a board, sieve a little icing sugar over and cut into small pieces. Keep in the fridge.

ANDY & HEATHER:
"These are delicious. Beware, once you start eating them, they are moreish."

Watch a video of melting chocolate at
noshbooks.com/melting-chocolate

yummy desserts

These are for special days and treats. We all love a good bit of indulgence and, so long as we don't have them every day, we can feel free to enjoy them. There are one or two old favourites and some new ideas too.

Fruit Crumble

NOTE: You can vary the filling. Use 3 apples and make it all apple, or use other frozen or fresh fruits.

2 medium **cooking apples**

500g packet **frozen fruits**, e.g. blueberries and strawberries

1 tablespoon **sugar**

¼ mug **water**

Crumble

1 mug **muesli**

1 mug/170g **flour**

100g **butter** (measure using packet)

2 tablespoons **sugar**

cream or **custard** to serve

1 Preheat the oven to 180ºC fan oven/200ºC/gas 6.

2 Peel and core the apples and cut into bite-sized chunks. Place in a saucepan with water. Bring to the boil and simmer gently for 3–4 minutes, until the apples begin to soften. Add the sugar and frozen fruit and simmer for 1 minute, or until the sugar has dissolved.

3 Pour the mixture into the bottom of an 18cm casserole dish. Set to one side.

4 Rub the butter into the flour with your fingers until it resembles breadcrumbs (use a food processor if you have one). Add the sugar and muesli and mix together.

5 Sprinkle evenly over the top of the fruit and press down gently. Cook in the oven for 20–25 minutes. The top should be golden brown.

Watch a video of rubbing butter into flour at
noshbooks.com/rubbing

Jelly Berry Trifle with Fresh Strawberries

300g pack of **fresh strawberries**

2 soft **trifle sponges**, pulled apart

1 packet **jelly, raspberry** or **strawberry**

2 mugs **water**

2 tablespoon **runny honey**

500ml tub of **Greek yogurt**

1 Take the tops off the strawberries and cut into bite-sized pieces. Place in the trifle bowl with the sponges.

2 Dissolve the jelly cubes in a mug of boiling water and then add the other 1 mug of cold water.

3 Pour the jelly over the fruit and sponges. Leave in the fridge for 2–3 hours until set.

4 Mix the honey into the yogurt and pour over the set jelly.

Raspberry Delight with Praline Shards

½ x 500g bag of **frozen raspberries**

4 ready-made **meringue nests**

300ml **double cream**

½ x 600ml pot **Greek yogurt**

Praline

1 mug **sugar**

½ mug **flaked almonds**

1 Make the praline by putting the sugar in a clean frying pan over a medium heat. Allow it to heat up gently and keep shaking the pan. Do not stir. Eventually the sugar will melt and go golden brown. Add the almonds and quickly spread the praline out onto a teflon sheet. Allow to cool and then break into shards. Set to one side until needed.

2 Put the raspberries in a bowl and break them up a bit.

3 Break up the meringue nests into chunks, not dust.

4 Whip the double cream until it begins to stiffen. Add the yoghurt.

5 Mix everything together, except the praline, and divide into 4–5 bowls. Leave in the fridge for a maximum of 2 hours, any more and the meringues will dissolve. Decorate with praline shards.

£0.40 /PERSON

Lime and Ginger Cheesecake

NOTE: You can change the ginger snaps for Hobnobs and the lime for lemon. This makes a wonderfully simple, lemon cheesecake.

ONE MORE THING: An easy way to remove the cake from the tin is to put a can (e.g. can of beans) under the cake tin and gently push down the sides of the cake tin, leaving the cake balanced on the can of beans.

200g packet of **ginger snaps**

100g **butter** (measure using packet), melted

300g pack of **cream cheese** (Philadelphia)

zest and juice of 3 **limes**

300ml **double cream**

3 heaped tablespoons **icing sugar**

1 Put the ginger snaps into a plastic bag and give them a good bash with a rolling pin, until they look like breadcrumbs.

2 Melt the butter and add the biscuit crumbs. Line a 20cm, loose-bottomed cake tin with greaseproof paper. Press the biscuit crumbs into the base.

3 Mix together the cream cheese, sugar, lime juice and rind until it is smooth. Mix with a whisk or electric beater if it goes lumpy.

4 Beat the cream in a separate bowl until it is stiff. Be careful not to make it into butter. Gently mix together with the cheese and lime. The lime juice will cause the cream to set and should begin to go thick as you mix it together.

5 Pour on top of the biscuit base and smooth out.

6 Place in the fridge for 2 hours.

DAVID & HANNAH: "I made this for a bigger group of people and they all enjoyed it. I thought it was delicious and easy to make."

Watch a video of how much to beat cream at
noshbooks.com/cream

Berry Cinnamon Torte

NOTE: If you like cinnamon you will love this. The cream, Greek yogurt and honey make a great alternative to just having cream.

175g **butter** (measure using packet), softened

²/₃ mug/180g **sugar**

3 **eggs**

1¹/₂ mugs/175g **ground almonds**

1 mug/170g **self-raising flour**

1 teaspoon ground **cinnamon**

2 tablespoons **water**

¹/₂ x 400g pack of **frozen berries** (e.g. summer fruits or raspberries), defrosted

icing sugar, for dusting

150ml **double cream**, whipped

150ml **Greek yogurt**

1 tablespoon **honey**

1 Preheat the oven to 180ºC fan oven/200ºC/ gas 6. Grease and line a 23cm cake tin.

2 Beat the butter and sugar together until light and fluffy. Add the eggs and beat well.

3 Add the almonds, flour, cinnamon and water and mix well.

4 Put half the mixture on the bottom of the cake tin and spread out. Spread the fruit over and then the rest of the torte mixture. It will spread out in the oven, so does not need to be too even.

5 Place in the oven for 40–45 minutes. It should be browned and risen. Once cooled, sift some icing sugar over the top.

6 Mix the honey with the yogurt and add to the whipped cream. Serve with the torte.

Watch a video of how much to beat cream at
noshbooks.com/cream

Apple Pie with Custard

NOTE: You can make the pastry in a food processor. Put the flour and butter in the processor and pulse a few times until it looks like breadcrumbs. Add the sugar and pulse once. Add the egg and about 3 tablespoons of water and pulse again. It should make a soft dough. Take out of the processor and squash together. Place in the fridge for ½ an hour.

Filling

3 large **Bramley apples**, peeled and cut into large chunks

³/₄ mug **water**

3 tablespoons **sugar**

1 teaspoon **mixed spice**

Pastry

150g **butter** (measure using packet)

1³/₄ mugs/300g **plain flour**

1 tablespoon **icing sugar**

1 **egg**, beaten

3 tablespoons **water**

1 beaten **egg** to brush the top

Custard

2 mugs **milk**

2 tablespoons **custard powder**

2 tablespoons **sugar**

1 teaspoon **vanilla extract**

1 Put the apples and the water in a pan and bring to the boil. Turn down to simmer, with a lid on the pan, for 3 minutes. The apples should be a bit "raggy" round the edges. Add the sugar and spice, and mix. Pour into a pie dish.

2 To make the pastry, rub in the butter and flour until it looks like breadcrumbs. Add the sugar and stir. Add the egg and enough water to make a soft dough. Squash together, cover with cling film and place in the fridge for ½ an hour.

3 Preheat the oven to 180ºC fan oven/200ºC/ gas 6.

4 Roll the pastry out and place over the apples. Trim the edges and pinch them to look pretty. Brush with the beaten egg and make a hole in the centre to let out the steam. Place in the oven for 25 minutes.

5 If you are making the custard, put the milk on to boil. Mix the custard powder and sugar together in a jug and add a little cold milk to mix it to a thin paste. Once the milk is boiling, add to the jug and stir quickly. If the custard does not thicken, place in the microwave for 30 seconds and then stir. Serve with the pie.

Watch a video of making pastry
noshbooks.com/pastry

Quick Apricot and Raspberry Trifles

300ml packet of **custard**

3–4 square **trifle sponges**

juice of an **orange** or 2 tablespoons of packet **orange juice**

400g tin **apricots**, drained and cut into ¼'s

100g **raspberries**

300ml **double cream**

¼ x 200g block of **white chocolate**, grated

1 Break up the sponges and place in the bottom of individual dishes. Divide the orange juice between them. Add the apricots and raspberries to the bowls.

2 Divide the custard between the bowls.

3 Whip the cream and place on top. Sprinkle the grated chocolate over the top.

Sticky Toffee Pudding with Hot Fudge Sauce

125g softened **butter** (measure using packet)

1 mug/210g **demarara** or **soft brown sugar**

3 **eggs**

1 tablespoon **golden syrup**

250g packet ready-to-eat **dates**, chopped

1²/₃ mugs/280g **self-raising flour**

2 **tablespoons water**

Fudge sauce

300ml carton **double cream**

1 tablespoon **golden syrup**

½ mug/105g **demarara** or **soft brown sugar**

50g **butter** (measure using packet)

1 teaspoon **vanilla** extract

1 Preheat the oven to 160ºC fan oven/180ºC/gas 4. Grease a 30x20cm dish (needs to be 5cm high).

2 Beat the butter and sugar. Add the eggs, one at a time, and beat well. Stir in the syrup.

3 Add the dates, flour and water and mix well. Pour into the dish and spread out. Place in the oven for 35–40 minutes.

4 To make the toffee sauce, put the butter, cream, syrup, sugar and butter into a saucepan and gently bring to the boil. Simmer until the sugar has dissolved. Add the vanilla extract. Serve with the hot pudding.

£ 0.71 /PERSON | SERVES 8 | EASE ★★★☆☆ | PREP 25 MINS | COOK 60 MINS | COOL 15 MINS | V GF

Almond Pear Pavlova with Chocolate Sauce

NOTE: This is best eaten the day that you make it. It goes very gooey by the next day, but, it is still very tasty.

ONE MORE THING: Don't be shy with the chocolate sauce with this one, there is nothing like excess!

Almond Meringue

4 **egg** whites

1 mug/225g **caster sugar**

100g packet **ground almonds**

Chocolate Sauce

100g bar **milk chocolate**

½ mug **double cream**

1 mug/300ml **double cream**, whipped

large tin **pears**, drained of juice

1 Preheat the oven to 150ºC fan oven/170ºC/gas 3. Put some greaseproof paper on a large baking tray.

2 Whisk the egg whites in a clean bowl until they form stiff peaks.

3 Gradually add the sugar and beat until the mixture is smooth and silky. It should be quite stiff.

4 Gently fold in the ground almonds.

5 Tip out onto the tray and spread the meringue into a 30cm round.

6 Put in the oven for 1 hour. After one hour, turn off the heat, but leave the meringue in for another 15 minutes. Take out of the oven; if you leave it in, it will continue to dry out.

7 Meanwhile, make the chocolate sauce. Put the cream in a small saucepan and bring to the boil. Take off the heat and add the broken-up chocolate. Stir until the chocolate melts. Leave to cool.

8 Once the meringue has cooled, put the whipped cream over the top. Place the drained pears on top of the cream. Drizzle the chocolate sauce over the top just before serving.

Watch a video of making pavlovas at
noshbooks.com/pavlova

index

A

almond pear pavlova with chocolate sauce 246
amazing wedges 19
american breakfast pancakes 92
apple and coconut sweet curry 56
apple and fennel salad 50
apple and pork stew 102
apple chutney 200
apple cinnamon muffins 226
apple pie with custard 242
apple salad 28,98
apricot and raspberry trifles 244
apricot flap jacks 223

B

bacon and beans jacket potato 22
bacon and beef bake 104
bacon and mozzarella pasta bake 34,69
bacon & banana sandwich 27
bacon & brie sandwich 27
balsamic chilli beef ragu 84
banana and nut muffins 226
banana and pecan nut cake 214
banana sandwich 27
bangers and sweet potato mash 35,136
barbeque chicken with apple salad 98
bean dip 156
beans on toast with egg on top 24
beef
  balsamic chilli beef ragu 84
  beef and bacon bake 104
  beef and mushroom casserole 124
  beef and mushroom pie with crispy potato top 194
  beef and potato hot-pot 72
  beef and tomato pie with potato crush 110
  beef burgers with crispy fried onions 168
  beef with cream cheese and sun-dried tomato sandwich 27
  ben's desperate dan cow pie 132
  corned beef hash with poached eggs 37,190
  easy shepherd's pie 135
  lasagna with added smoky bacon 138
  masala mince 185
  mini meat loaves 152
  one-pot beef cobbler 37,122
  pastitsio 204
  simple beef curry 125
  spaghetti bolognese 134
  steak and ale casserole 142
  stew and suet dumplings 128
beef and bacon bake 104
beef and mushroom casserole 124
beef and mushroom pie with crispy potato top 194
beef and potato hot-pot 72
beef and tomato pie with potato crush 110
beef burgers with crispy fried onions 168
beef cobbler 37,122
beef curry 125
beef ragu 84
beef with cream cheese and sun-dried tomato sandwich 27
beetroot salad 156
ben's desperate dan cow pie 132
berry cinnamon torte 240
berry trifle with fresh strawberries 236
blueberry muffins 226
blueberry pancakes with caramel sauce 95
bolognese 134
breakfast pancakes 92
brie & bacon sandwich 27
burgers with crispy fried onions 168
butterfly cakes 228
butternut squash soup 48

C

cajun chicken wrap 175
caramel sauce 95
carrot and apple salad 28
carrot and leek soup 43
carrot cake tray bake 212
carrot salad 108
casserole 142
celery, fennel and apple salad 29
chapatis 114
cheddar and mustard mash 20
cheese and herb salmon 151
cheese and onion patties with apple chutney 200
cheesecake 238
cheese on toast 24
cheese pinwheels 41
chestnut patties 172
chicken
  barbeque chicken with apple salad 98
  cajun chicken wrap 175
  chicken and leek pie 130
  chicken & bacon wrap 175
  chicken burgers 170
  chicken chapatis 114
  chicken, mayo & lettuce sandwich 27
  chicken nuggets and wedges 37,162,180
  chicken quesadillas and tomato salsa 176
  chicken tetrazzini 78
  cooked chicken and mayonnaise jacket potato 22
  creamy chicken and mushroom pie 60
  creamy tomato chicken 80
  fennel chicken pasta 62
  ginger chicken stir-fry 76
  honey chicken bake 64
  honey sesame chicken with carrot salad 108
  lemon couscous salad 74

lemon ginger chicken 150
moroccan honey chicken 58
one-pot chicken hot pot 188
one-pot chicken korma 36,82
roast chicken dinner 140
spiced chicken & herb couscous 154
thai coconut chicken 148
chicken and leek pie 130
chicken and mayonnaise jacket potato 22
chicken and mushroom pie 60
chicken & bacon wrap 175
chicken bake 64
chicken burgers 170
chicken chapatis 114
chicken dinner 140
chicken & herb couscous 154
chicken hot pot 188
chicken korma rice 36,82
chicken, mayo & lettuce sandwich 27
chicken nuggets and wedges 37,162,180
chicken pasta 62
chicken quesadillas and tomato salsa 176
chicken stir-fry 76
chicken tetrazzini 78
chicken with apple salad 98
chicken with carrot salad 108
chicken wrap 175
chilli beef ragu 84
chocolate and maple muffins 226
chocolate chip cookies 224
chocolate chip muffins 226
chocolate oat cookies 216
chocolate sauce 246
chorizo and pancetta bake 35,70
cinnamon muffins 226
cinnamon torte 240
coconut chicken 148
coconut poached thai chicken 68
coconut sweet curry 56
coffee shop cookies 220
cooked chicken and mayonnaise 22
cooked chicken and mayonnaise jacket potato 22

cookies 210,215,220,224
corned beef hash with poached eggs 37,190
cottage cheese & banana sandwich 27
courgette fritters with feta salad 186
couscous salad 29
couscous salad 74
cow pie 132
cream cheese and sun-dried tomato sandwich 27
creamy chicken and mushroom pie 60
creamy tomato chicken 80
crispy fried lamb 81
crispy topped vegetable bake 192
crumble 234
crunchy topped tuna bake 86
cucumber pickle 146
cumberland hot dogs with tomato salsa 184
curried lamb burgers & mango salad 169

D

date and nut bars 208
desperate dan cow pie 132
dumplings 128

E

easy shepherd's pie 135
egg and smoked salmon bake 198
egg-fried ploughman's 94
egg mayo sandwich 27
egg & salmon wrap 175

F

fairy cakes 228
fennel and apple salad 29
fennel chicken pasta 62
feta salad 186
fish

crunchy topped tuna bake 86
egg & salmon wrap 175
grilled tuna bagels 35,40
gruyère and herb salmon 151
healthy fish and chips 137
hoisin and sesame tuna noodles 37,52
mackerel pâté 156
oriental egg and smoked salmon bake 198
poached salmon with mustard sauce and cucumber pickle 146
salmon and soured cream jacket potato 22
salmon cakes with hoisin dip 96
salmon on toast 24
smoked salmon and cream cheese spaghetti 36,193
smoked salmon & cream cheese sandwich 27
super simple tuna bake 171
tuna & hard-boiled egg sandwich 27
tuna on toast 24
tuna, sweetcorn and mayo jacket potato 22
fish and chips 137
fish cakes with hoisin dip 96
flap jacks 223
fried ploughman's 94
fritters with feta salad 186
fruit crumble 234
fry-up 90
fudge sauce 245

G

garlic olives 156
ginger cheesecake 238
ginger chicken 150
ginger chicken stir-fry 76
green salad with croutons 29
grilled tuna bagels 35,40
gruyère and herb salmon 151

H

ham and cheese pinwheels 41

hash with poached eggs 37,190
healthy fish and chips 137
herb couscous 154
herb salmon 151
hoisin and sesame tuna noodles
37,52
hoisin dip 96
honey, carrot and leek soup 43
honey chicken 58
honey chicken bake 64
honey sesame chicken with carrot
salad 108
hot dogs with tomato salsa 184
hot-pot 72,188
hummus 156

J

jacket potatoes 22
jacket potato with crispy fried
lamb 81
jelly berry trifle with fresh strawberries 236

K

korma rice 36,82

L

lamb
   crispy fried lamb 81
   curried lamb burgers & mango
   salad 169
   lamb meatballs with sweet
   potato rice 116
   moroccan lamb pie 35,100
lamb burgers & mango salad 169
lamb meatballs with sweet potato
rice 116
lamb pie 35,100
lasagna with added smoky bacon
138
leek pie 130
leek soup 43
lemon couscous salad 74
lemon ginger chicken 150
lentil soup 42

lime and ginger cheesecake 238
lunch box cookies 215

M

mackerel pâté 156
mango salad 169
maple muffins 226
masala mince 185
mash 20
meat and potato pie 132
meatballs 178
meatballs with sweet potato
rice 116
meat loaves 152
melting moments 222
mezze 156
millionaire's shortbread 218
mini meat loaves 152
mini roast potatoes 18
minty potato salad 28
moroccan honey chicken 58
moroccan lamb pie 35,100
mozzarella pasta bake 34,69
mozzarella stuffed tomatoes 49
muffins 226
mug 10
mushroom and pork stew 35,112
mushroom casserole 124
mushroom omelette with apple
and fennel salad 50
mushroom pie with crispy potato
top 194
mustard mash 20
mustard sauce and cucumber
pickle 146

N

nuggets and wedges 37,162,180
nut bars 208
nut cake 214

O

oat cookies 216
omelette with apple and fennel
salad 50

one-pot beef cobbler 37,122
one-pot chicken hot pot 188
one-pot chicken korma 36,82
one-pot sausage meatballs 178
onion patties with apple chutney
200
orange cookies 210
oriental egg and smoked salmon
bake 198

P

pancakes 92
pancakes with caramel sauce 95
pastitsio 204
pastry 33
patties 172
patties with apple chutney 200
pavlova with chocolate sauce
246
pear pavlova with chocolate
sauce 246
pecan nut cake 214
pinwheels 41
ploughman's 94
poached salmon with mustard
sauce and cucumber pickle 146
poached thai chicken 68
pork
   bacon and mozzarella pasta
   bake 34,69
   bacon & brie sandwich 27
   bangers and sweet potato mash
   35,136
   beef and bacon bake 104
   chorizo and pancetta bake
   35,70
   creamy pork and mushroom
   stew 35,112
   cumberland hot dogs with
   tomato salsa 184
   ham and cheese pinwheels 41
   lasagna with added smoky
   bacon 138
   one-pot sausage meatballs 178
   salami and red pepper jacket
   potato 22
   sausage and chestnut patties
   172

sausage and veg traybake 36,196
sausage stew with borlotti beans 202
scrumpy pork pie 106
simple saturday brunch 90
slow-cook roast pork 120
sweet pork and apple stew 102
toad in the hole with cox's apples 126
pork and apple stew 102
pork and mushroom stew 35,112
pork pie 106
posh roast potatoes 19
potato crush 20
potato hot-pot 72
potato salad 28
praline 237

Q

quesadillas and tomato salsa 176
quick apricot and raspberry trifles 244

R

ragu 84
raspberry delight with praline shards 237
raspberry or blueberry muffins 226
raspberry trifles 244
red pepper jacket potato 22
rice salad 28
roast chicken dinner 140
roasted sweet potato soup 13,44
roast pork 120
roast potatoes 19
roast potatoes 18
rocky road 230

S

salads 28
salami and red pepper jacket potato 22
salmon and cream cheese spa-

ghetti 36,193
salmon and soured cream jacket potato 22
salmon bake 198
salmon cakes with hoisin dip 96
salmon on toast 24
salmon with mustard sauce and cucumber pickle 146
salmon wrap 175
sandwiches 27
sausage and chestnut patties 172
sausage and veg traybake 36,196
sausage meatballs 178
sausage stew with borlotti beans 202
scrambled eggs & cheese and tomato sandwich 27
scrumpy pork pie 106
sesame chicken with carrot salad 108
sesame tuna noodles 37,52
shepherd's pie 135
shortbread 218
simple beef curry 125
simple saturday brunch 90
slow-cook roast pork 120
smoked salmon and cream cheese spaghetti 36,193
smoked salmon bake 198
smoked salmon & cream cheese sandwich 27
soured cream jacket potato 22
spaghetti bolognese 134
spiced apricot turkey burgers 37,166
spiced chicken & herb couscous 154
spicy butternut squash soup 48
squash soup 48
steak and ale casserole 142
stew and suet dumplings 128
sticky toffee pudding with hot fudge sauce 245
stuffed tomatoes 49
suet dumplings 128
sun-dried tomato sandwich 27
sun-dried tomato soup with parmesan toast 46
super simple tuna bake 171

sweetcorn and mayo jacket potato 22
sweet pork and apple stew 102
sweet potato and lentil soup 42
sweet potato jacket potato 22
sweet potato mash 20
sweet potato mash 35,136
sweet potato rice 116
sweet potato soup 13,44

T

thai chicken 68
thai coconut chicken 148
toad in the hole with cox's apples 126
toffee pudding with hot fudge sauce 245
tomato chicken 80
tomato pie with potato crush 110
tomato salsa 184
tomato salsa 176
tomato soup with parmesan toast 46
torte 240
tray bake 212
trifles 244
trifle with fresh strawberries 236
tuna bagels 35,40
tuna bake 86,171
tuna & hard-boiled egg sandwich 27
tuna noodles 37,52
tuna on toast 24
tuna, sweetcorn and mayo jacket potato 22
turkey burgers 37,166

V

vegetable bake 192
veg traybake 36,196

W

wedges 19
wraps 174

say hello to all our families...

David & Hannah

We have 3 little girls, Eve 5, Faith 4 and Beth 2. As well as looking after the girls, Hannah works part-time as a GP receptionist and David is a teacher at the local school. Fresh and healthy food is important to us, as is being adventurous. We love recipes that are quick to make and in keeping with our food budget.

Ben & Nicole

We have 3 kids, Isabella (4), Toby (2) and Poppy (1). Nicole, a full time mum, while Ben runs his own business. We love good food with minimal fuss. If I even mutter the words "Chicken Pie" Isabella get's crazy excited. I think she might love it more than the colour pink... well...maybe not...but it is a close second!

Lee & Sarah

We are a family with 4 'full of beans' young kids (Jack 2, Lily-May 3, Callum 6, & Emma 8), a husband who seems to be a bigger kid than them all and Sarah a full time mum. We live in Bedford, since relocating from London around 10 years ago. We all enjoy spending time together with friends & visiting new places.

Peter & Bernice

Not sure what you call off-spring who are 18+, sometimes at home and sometimes not, but we have 3 of these (Josh, Bethany and Ben), plus 1–2 lodgers, so the numbers eating can vary widely. To further complicate catering, the above mix includes veggies, omnivores, carnivores, and some "fussy-vores". Dishes which are quick to prepare,, exciting to the taste buds, AND economical, are particularly welcome.

Dan & Leena

We have 3 young boys, Elijah 5, Aaron 4 and Aidan 2. Leena is a full-time stay-at-home mum and Dan works as a social worker. We all love our food and enjoy cooking and eating foods from different countries. At this stage of our lives, days can be very hectic and it would be useful to have recipes that are convenient to prepare and cook, but are also tasty and appealing for all of us.

Steve & Candy

Jessica and Joel love spending time with each other, especially around a table of tasty food. Jessica enjoys helping to bake, especially cracking eggs open! Joel enjoys rough and tumbling with his Dad. One of our favourite 'Joy' recipes is "Spicy Moroccan Lamb Pie"; quick and super tasty.

Gary & Nikki

We have 3 young children, Emily 4, Naomi 7 and Ethan 9. Life is very busy as a family. Gary works long shifts in London and Nikki is a play leader at a local Pre-School, so not a lot of time to cook. We all love to sit down as a family, but this can be difficult with Gary doing shifts. So looking for easy and quick meals that can be cooked and enjoyed as a family.

Jo

I am a busy single mum who works full-time. I have two children, Emily 15 and Oliver 12. We all love to cook and enjoy food with lots of flavour, but that doesn't take too long to get to the plate.

Joe & Sarah

We have 2 young boys, Seth (6) and Jared (4). Both are always hungry! Cooking for our family needs to be fun, not too time consuming, but yet provide a healthy, hearty meal for us all to enjoy.

Andy & Heather

We have 5 children, Joanna 21, Daniel 19, Bethany 16, Rachel 16 and Nathan 14. 4 of them still live at home and have very healthy appetites. We all like trying different food and, with busy lives, we've found the recipes in this book great, for variety, speed and economy.

Alan & Jo

We are the Layton family: Alan, Jo and grown up children Sam, Rosie and Charlie. We are all very busy, Alan and Jo both working full-time. We love cooking and sharing meals as a family and with our friends. Meals in our house have to be very flexible and elastic, as we are never quite sure who will be in and how many extra people there might be. We loved trying out the recipes, especially gaining lots of new ideas.

Luke & Rachel

We have 2 young girls, Samantha is 2 and a half (and loves playing outdoors) and Melody is 1 (and loves playing with her musical giraffe!). They're lots of fun and keep Rach busy at home, whilst Luke goes out to work with young people. Our family love food and love eating together! We both enjoy cooking, but it can be hard to find time in the day to prepare delicious, healthy food and also to find and try out new recipes. So we're looking forward to some new ideas and inspiration!

Adam & Connie

In our family, we have Adam, who's a teacher, myself as full-time Mum and two little girls, Molly 3 and Esme 21 months. Food is a definite pleasure in our household, but fresh ideas do not always come easily. Meals are prepared often in a rush and can be fairly repetitive. Food that is full of flavour and easy to make are the sort of recipes we love.

conversions

All of these are approximate conversions, which have either been rounded up or down. Never mix metric and imperial measures in one recipe; stick to one system or the other.

Temperature

Gas	Fan ºC	Oven ºC	Oven ºF
1	120	140	275
2	130	150	300
3	150	170	325
4	160	180	350
5	170	190	375
6	180	200	400
7	200	220	425
8	210	230	450
9	220	240	475

Weight

Metric	Imperial
15g	½ oz
20g	¾ oz
25g	1 oz
40g	1 ½ oz
50g	2 oz
70g	2 ½ oz
75g	3 oz
100g	4 oz
150g	5 oz
175g	6 oz
200g	7 oz
225g	8 oz
250g	9 oz
275g	10 oz
350g	12 oz
450g	1 lb
675g	1 ½ lb
900g	2 lb
1.35kg	3 lb

Volume

Metric	Imperial
25ml	1 fl oz
50ml	2 fl oz
85ml	3 fl oz
150ml	5 fl oz (¼ Pint)
300ml	10 fl oz (½ Pint)
450ml	15 fl oz (¾ Pint)
600ml	1 Pint
1 litre	1 ¾ Pints
1.2 litres	2 Pints
1.5 litres	2 ½ Pints
2 litres	3 ½ Pints
2.25 litres	4 Pints
2.75 litres	5 Pints
4.5 litres	8 Pints (1 Gallon)

Length

Metric	Imperial
0.5 cm	¼ inch
1 cm	½ inch
2.5 cm	1 inch
5 cm	2 inches
7.5 cm	3 inches
10 cm	4 inches
15 cm	6 inches
18 cm	7 inches
20 cm	8 inches
23 cm	9 inches
25 cm	10 inches
30 cm	12 inches

cooking times

boiling vegetables

Swedes and turnips	2–3cm chunks	20–25 mins
Potatoes	2–3cm chunks	10–15 mins
Parsnips, carrots	cut into 2cm rings	10–15 mins
Cauliflower	broken into little trees	10 mins
Broccoli	broken into little trees	5 mins
Green beans	cut off the stalk and tail	5 mins
Spinach	take off any thick stalks	30 secs–1 min
Leeks	cut into 2cm rings	5 mins
Cabbage	cut into long thin strips	5 mins
Sugar snaps	leave as they are	2 mins
Mangetout	leave as they are	1 min

roasting vegetables

Potatoes	cut into 5–6cm chunks	40–50 mins
Butternut squash	peel, cut into 5–6cm chunks	30–40 mins
Parsnips	cut into 4, lengthways	40–45 mins
Sweet potatoes	peel, cut into 5–6cm chunks	40–50 mins
Onions	cut into 6 wedges	40–50 mins
Fennel	cut into 4 wedges	30–40 mins
Tomatoes	cut the skin	20–25 mins
Peppers	remove seeds & stalk, cut into large pieces	25 mins

the nosh family

Nosh Books began when B
went to uni. He couldn't coo
wouldn't cook! Only when th
realities of uni dawned, and
realised how hungry he was,
he begin to show an interest.
we wrote "Nosh for Students"
that was 11 years ago. Ben car
cook now; he has a young fam
and often needs to cook. This
our 5th book and we are really
excited about it, because we fee
that the contents are just what

busy mums and dads need. We have loved producing it together. I do the cooking an
research, Tim does the photography and helps with the research, Ben does the desig
and graphics and Ron makes sure we are all doing it right and not going too far off
the wall! We do, of course, all have a say in what the other is doing! Everyone gets
involved in the tasting and testing. Ben and Tim are great cooks and great critics, Ron
just loves eating. Together, this is a recipe for lots of fun and lively interaction.

thanks

A special thanks to all our volunteer families for testing all of our recipes for us, we
really appreciate it.

Thanks to my very good friend Fran Maciver for proofreading the book.
Bella's tea party - thanks to Bella, Grace, Ella, Hannah, Evie, Faith, Beth and Toby.
Teens' video night - thanks to Sam, Bethany, Jemima, Rachel and Nathan.
Getting kids involved - thanks to Ollie and Emily.

Printed in China
Published by: inTRADE (GB) ltd.
Contact: joymay@mac.com
Author: Joy May

1st edition: September 2017
ISBN: 9780993260957
Photography and Artwork: Tim May
@ www.milkbottlephotography.co.uk
Design: Ben May
@ www.milkbottledesigns.co.uk
Visit us @ www.noshbooks.com
Proofreading: Fran Maciver
Editor: Ron May